The Call of the Mourning Dove

The Call of the Mourning Dove

How Sacred Sound Awakens Mystical Unity

STEPHANIE RUTT

Foreword by S. Mark Heim

RESOURCE *Publications* • Eugene, Oregon

THE CALL OF THE MOURNING DOVE
How Sacred Sound Awakens Mystical Unity

Copyright © 2019 Stephanie Rutt. All rights reserved. Except for brief quotations in critical publications or reviews, no part of this book may be reproduced in any manner without prior written permission from the publisher. Write: Permissions, Wipf and Stock Publishers, 199 W. 8th Ave., Suite 3, Eugene, OR 97401.

Resource Publications
An Imprint of Wipf and Stock Publishers
199 W. 8th Ave., Suite 3
Eugene, OR 97401

www.wipfandstock.com

PAPERBACK ISBN: 978-1-5326-6113-6
HARDCOVER ISBN: 978-1-5326-6114-3
EBOOK ISBN: 978-1-5326-6115-0

Manufactured in the U.S.A. MAY 8, 2019

Scripture quotations are from the New Revised Standard Version Bible: Anglicized Edition, copyright © 1989, 1995 National Council of the Churches of Christ in the United States of America. Used by permission. All rights reserved worldwide.

To all those who have felt they could not

Contents

Foreword by S. Mark Heim / ix
Preface / xi
Acknowledgments / xv
The Sound of God / xvii
Introduction / xix

PART 1   The Call: Echoes Sounding a New Day / 1
         1   A Cry for Unity / 3
         2   Harmonic Preludes / 10

PART 2   Answering the Call: The Sonic Trilogy of Love / 25
         3   The Crucible of Transcendence / 27
         4   *Lover*: Practitioner / 37
         5   *Love*: Sacred Sound / 46
         6   *Beloved*: God / 65

PART 3   Living the Call: Awakened Mystical Unity / 81
         7   Sounding Our Note / 83
         8   The Divine Chorus / 95
            Conclusion / 109

Bibliography / 113
Index / 121

Foreword

IT IS A PLEASURE to write these few words of commendation and introduction for Stephanie Rutt's new work, *The Call of the Mourning Dove*. I came to know Stephanie during her time at Andover Newton Theological School, when she was a student in my classes. Though I knew her first as a passionate and creative student, those who read this book will quickly appreciate that she is also a consummate teacher. She combines to an extraordinary degree breadth of vision, spiritual humility, and a profound, humane energy. These qualities draw her continually into interfaith exploration and at the same time draw others to her in appreciation of that common search. She has become a leader in developing a free-standing, free range program of study and practice for kindred spirits. This book makes that project accessible to a wider circle.

The hallmark of Stephanie's approach is its concreteness. She approaches religious traditions not primarily through their lofty thoughts or their structural organization but through points where they intersect with our bodies and our senses. Most particularly, here, she approaches them through sound. What might seem like the most elementary and preliminary steps—-learning to speak the simple, first confession of Muslim faith or to say the most common of Christian prayers—become Rosetta stones that unlock new vistas of transformation. Her work on the spiritual inbreaking that takes place when one prays a prayer in its original language blends the mystical meaning of sound with the human

Foreword

quest for connection across times and spaces. In that way, what she creates is truly something new.

Stephanie Rutt's work is an inspiring intersection of concrete spiritual practice, inter-religious learning and pastoral sensitivity. *The Call of the Mourning Dove* continues a pioneering path, in which common human modalities of sound, speech and body become avenues for personal renewal and reconciliation across communities. There is wisdom here that can be applied within our existing religious congregations as well as among the seeking and the unaffiliated.

S. MARK HEIM
Samuel Abbot Professor of Christian Theology
Andover Newton Seminary at Yale Divinity School

Preface

I ALWAYS KNEW GOD was right where I couldn't quite see. I knew because I could hear him through those slightly off-key voices singing loud and unencumbered to the old piano in my hometown church. I saw him in the eyes of that homeless man, the one with the sign, looking at me as I nervously waited for the stoplight to change. I could feel him shaking in the fingers of the elderly clerk, reaching from behind the counter, giving me change at the corner five and dime.

So, when I went in search of God, I didn't go first to books or lectures or to hear more sermons. I didn't want to learn *about* God. I didn't want an intermediary. No. I wanted my own unmitigated experience of God. So, instead, I sought out teachers from a variety of faith traditions and asked each to teach me how to find God. With guidance and support, I took to my prayer mat and began to fervently pray intoning the sacred practices from the ancient cannons. And, along the way, I did indeed, most graciously, find God, again and again, right where I would have never thought to look—waiting right there in the silence—just beyond my understanding.

I found God's amazing grace, knowing fully *I once was lost but now I'm found,* and came to feel him intimately as my treasure as the hymn *Be Thou My Vision* proclaimed. Many years later, I would come to know his hallowed name, unrefined, in the depths of the Lord's Prayer in Aramaic. I sensed him in the sweet emptiness of contemplative prayer and discovered him walking with me *through the valley of the shadow of death* as the Hebrew Alpha-Beis

Preface

became a lamp onto my feet. I felt him dancing inside my soul as I chanted the beautiful Sikh practice *Kal Akal*. And, he had brought me to stillness while turning, turning, turning with the Sufis leaving no doubt of my unity with all from my moving breathing practice of *la ilaha illa allah*. He held me fast as I endured purification in the Native American sweat lodges as he guided me to new vistas on the sound of the Shaman's drum. In *Vipassana* meditation, he showed me definitively the difference between my thinking about him and knowing him. And from the *Om Mani Padma Hum* I came to know the jewel, alive and well, in the heart of the lotus echoing through the Bhagavad Gita, the song of God. Intoning the ancient practices in their original languages, across faith traditions, brought me, again and again, to the same portal leaving me silent, humble and filled with awe—at the feet of God—the same God—showing me definitively, graciously, that indeed, *many are the ways we pray to him*.

The new paradigm, the *Sonic Trilogy of Love*, explored in this book, represents most succinctly this discovery. "How can this be?" you may ask as faith traditions surely hold varying ontological beliefs about the nature of God. True. Yet, as those who've long explored one particular tradition, as well as those who are exploring across traditions, enter into the *Sonic Trilogy of Love* to intone the ancient practices, each creates the conditions for an unmitigated experience of God. In this way, the *Sonic Trilogy of Love* becomes a paradigm of unification, capable of holding the healthy tension that exists between particularity defining religious difference and the ubiquitous mystical experience engendering religious unity. The *Sonic Trilogy of Love* invites all seekers, one and all, home.

This is beautifully illustrated by theologian S. Mark Heim, who has graciously written the Forward for this book, in his article, "The Pluralism of Religious Ends Dreams Fulfilled." There he writes of his response to Gandhi's reflection, "Religions are different roads converging to the same point. What does it matter if we take different roads so long as we reach the same goal?" Heim counters, "What if religions are paths to different ends that they

PREFACE

each value supremely? Why should we object?"[1] To both Gandhi and Heim, I would answer, "And what if both of you are right?"

Today, as I continue to travel those roads to which Gandhi was referring, I never cease to marvel at the ways God makes himself known. So, I find myself in complete resonance with Heim's sentiment, "I am quite convinced that behind each tradition in principle there lies something of this same order of otherness and wonder."[2] To this, my heart can only reply, "Amen."

---

1. Heim, "Pluralism of Religious Ends," para 8.
2. Heim, "Otherness and Wonder," 196.

Acknowledgements

THIS BOOK WOULD NOT have been possible without Dr. Sarah B. Drummond who *heard* early on what was possible and with discerning enthusiasm pointed me in the direction of my heart's deepest knowing. There are no words adequate to express what a blessed gift this was in supporting me to step into the fullness of what I felt God was asking. Like a seasoned maestro, she encouraged me to sound my note in the divine symphony and bring forth a new melody seeking expression. Hence, the *Sonic Trilogy of Love* was born. There is no greater gift.

And just as Dr. Drummond made all possible, Dr. Jennifer Howe Peace helped to make the full expression of this new melody ring strong, clear, and true with her spaciousness of heart and laser tuning. Each step along the way, she guided and supported, questioned and affirmed, enabling this final song to be all it could be. Finally, Dr. Peace, in response to my reflecting upon a propensity to infuse the poetic with the scholarly, said simply, "Perhaps God sends the lovers." Graciously, this phrase freed me to use my full voice in these pages.

In addition, I would like to extend special thanks to Rev. Laurie Van Dyck for her many hours of proof reading and for offering valuable suggestions and feedback as one deeply familiar with both the history and depth of the work. Also, my enduring gratitude goes out to the many members of the Tree of Life Interfaith Temple community who studied the text, between thesis and book form, who also offered helpful reflections as only those who had truly experienced the work, over many years, could.

Acknowledgements

And, finally, I would like to acknowledge and thank my husband Doug for all his unwavering support, encouragement, and patient persevering throughout the long months of focus on this project. Reading every draft, he consistently offered feedback and inspired discussion helping me to bring the work into greater focus. On a daily basis, his presence and contributions, made all the difference.

The Sound of God

I recognize the feeling.

Caught.

Breathless.

Remembering. Forgetting.

Some unexpected and unforeseen yearning fulfilled.

Suspended from knowing.

Free falling, yet cradled, into the sweet abyss of unknowing.

I have been here before . . . when I first echoed the . . .

    Gayatri mantra in Sanskrit

        Kal Akal mantra in Gurmukhi

            Allah Ya Jamil mantra in Arabic

                Lord's Prayer in Aramaic

                    Psalm 23 in Hebrew.

The Sound of God

Last sounds before sleep.

First sounds upon waking.

And, each day carving deeper and deeper.

And each time...

I can't remember how I was when I began and I don't know where I may land.

For, like a bell echoes on the summer's breeze, each sound calls me home

and, together, they sing to me softly, chiming in the wind...

A kind of lullaby known only to the Beloved.

And, I... I am rocked to sleep... even as I am waking...

Rev. Stephanie Rutt, 2012

Introduction

Bless us with a divine voice
that we may tune the harp strings of our life
to sing songs of Love to you.
INSPIRED BY THE RIG VEDA

CHANGE IS IN THE wind. Western attitudes about religion, about God, have been steadily evolving led, in part, by a new demographic of seekers who describe their world view as "spiritual," not "religious."[1] No longer content to be passive recipients of the same liturgies, sermons, and homilies, no longer invested in the rituals gone rote, these "spiritual but not religious" seekers are leaving on a quest for God. Aspiring ministerial leaders and concerned lay people alike would do well to embrace this change as I believe it is an opportunity to reignite relevance, meaning and passion. As the great philosopher Rabindranath Tagore reminded us, "The winds of grace are always blowing, but it is you who must raise your sails."[2] It is time.

Where to begin? One way is already in the very hands of religious leaders and lay people alike, so close, perhaps, they may have missed it. Right there, within the rich texture of the historical

---

1. Murphy, "Emergence of Evolutionary Panentheism," 191.
2. Tagore, *Hinduism Today*, 14.

Introduction

"religious" canon, lie the very practices that can serve as the portal into the "spiritual" connection these modern-day seekers are craving. Christians may find this portal when mentally engaging a sacred word or phrase in the depths of contemplative prayer practice. Jews may find it when reciting portions of the Torah or the Psalms in Hebrew. Muslims may find it when chanting the ninety-nine beautiful names of Allah in Arabic. And of course, Hindus, Buddhists, and Sikhs, to name just a few, have long found it when chanting their sacred texts in mantra meditation. The common denominator? Sound.

As seekers across faith traditions engage the *sound* of God in spiritual practice, each may enter the portal into their own unmitigated experience of the divine. Whether mentally engaging a sacred word in contemplative prayer or chanting aloud according to an ancient script, the fruits of practice begin to answer a longing, a not-so-silent cry within, as the sound of God reverberates through the inner chambers, tuning and awakening seekers to that which was previously unknown. Wondrously, if only in passing moments, seekers may start to get just a glimpse of that which is beyond understanding, to suddenly see themselves as God sees them. And if so, nothing is the same.

In this book, I offer a new paradigm based on this sonic aspect of the divine, the *Sonic Trilogy of Love*, that explores just how sacred sound becomes the portal into this unmitigated experience of God. Here, identifying love as the core organizing principle, I describe the inter-relational dynamics between us, the *Lovers*, practitioners; the *Love*, sacred sound; and the *Beloved*, God. As the *Lover*, practitioner, engages the *Love*, sacred sound emanating from the sacred canon, conditions are set for unity with the *Beloved*, God. In such moments, the distinctions between the *Lover*, *Love* and *Beloved* dissolve in mystical unity. Finally, I show how such an experience, awakening personal transcendence within, engenders a sense of mystical unity without, embracing all creation.

Introduction

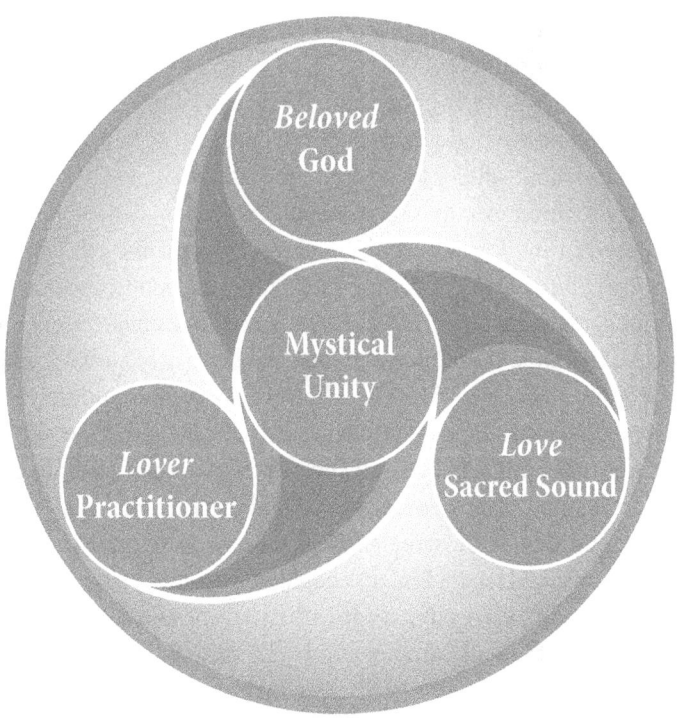

Part 1, "The Call: Echoes Sounding a New Day," begins with a chapter titled "A Cry for Unity," in which I address this current longing by the "spiritual but not religious" using the analogy of the mourning dove. I examine the cry for unity from the human and divine perspectives, revealing the origins of tension between those immersed in one faith tradition, whom I call the "traditionally religious," and those exploring across faith traditions, self-identifying as "spiritual but not religious." Finally, I introduce the *Sonic Trilogy of Love* as a unifying paradigm. Chapter 2, "Harmonic Preludes," explores the theological underpinnings now ripe to support this current quest for God. Rooted in perennial philosophy, it is found in the philosophical worldview called panentheism, at present unfamiliar to many scholars and most practitioners.[3] Ultimately,

---

3. Clayton, "Panentheism in the Tapestry," 201.

INTRODUCTION

panentheism describes theologically what the *Sonic Trilogy of Love* offers experientially.

Part 2, "Answering the Call: *The Sonic Trilogy of Love*," discusses this new paradigm in depth. Chapter 3, "The Crucible of Transcendence," discusses the unique structure of the trifold paradigm citing examples across faith traditions, defines *Love* as it is used in this context, and, finally, I highlight the critical role of silence, in relation to sound, in creating the conditions for the unmitigated experience of God. The next three chapters explore each of the three components in the *Sonic Trilogy of Love*. Chapter 4, "*Lover*: Practitioner," discusses how we create the conditions for personal transcendence and navigate the challenges inherent on the spiritual path. Chapter 5, "*Love*: Sacred Sound," outlines just what it is that makes a sound sacred and explores the roots of sacred sound across four sample faith traditions: Judaism, Hinduism, Christianity, and Islam. Finally, chapter 6, "*Beloved*: God," explores the nature of God through a panentheistic lens and highlights examples from the four sample faith traditions, illustrating how the *experience* of the sound of God engenders a sense of mystical unity with all peoples.

Part 3, "Living the Call: Awakened Mystical Unity," begins with chapter 7, "Sounding Our Note," focusing on the personal journey of the *Lover* in cultivating joy, clarity, gratitude, and surrender as the sound of God finds its ultimate expression in the experiences of daily life. Finally, in chapter 8, "The Divine Chorus," I explore the key sacred sound practices, from the four sample faith traditions, showing how each invokes a sense of mystical oneness.

A word about the selection of the four faith traditions highlighted: Judaism to include kabbalistic thought, Hinduism, Christianity, and Islam to include contributions from Sufism. I chose Judaism and Hinduism for their ancient roots in the historical canon as well as because, generally, they represent Western and Eastern views, respectively. I chose Christianity as it represents the predominant faith tradition in our national locale. And, finally, I chose Islam as it represents the most recent of the major world

INTRODUCTION

religions as well as the final, integral addition to the Abrahamic traditions.

My use of "he" and "him" in reference to God, the *Beloved*, bears explanation. As the focus is on the sacred sound practices from the ancient canons, I have chosen to align my textual language with the masculine pronouns inherent, or often implied, in those practices and which, traditionally, have been used in associated commentaries. Certainly, in moments of mystical unity within the *Sonic Trilogy of Love*, practitioners discover that God is not only utterly void of gender but, graciously, beyond all that can be described or articulated by human reasoning.

PART 1

The Call
Echoes Sounding a New Day

I

A Cry for Unity

In my longing I call out, "Is there anyone there?
I know each one is He, but in my heart there turns a tear;
when from men and rocks and trees plead "feel us, see us."
Beloved, lend me your eyes!
ABRAHAM JOSHUA HESCHEL[1]

THE CALL OF THE mourning dove is distinctive. Some might even say haunting. Yet unmistakable. One senses a kind of longing in the sound which, in the most concrete sense, is confirmed by our knowledge that the familiar *cooing* is elicited by the male in search of a mate, one who will join him in a monogamous partnership for life. Metaphorically, the dove is often cited as a symbol of the Holy Spirit particularly within the Christian tradition. The call, one could say, is God's love for us calling us home to be with him. We respond because the call answers some deep longing, perhaps

---

1. Hooper, *Hymns to the Beloved*.

indistinguishable, yet fully present, within us. We sense we will never be complete, whole, until we are united with our God.

It is this longing that is sending the "spiritual but not religious" on their quest for God. As Rabbi Heschel expressed in the quote above, they want to *feel* God, to have an experience of that which waits just beyond their understanding. And they want to be *seen* as well as to *see*. They want what Meister Eckhart expressed by saying, "The eye in which I see God is the same eye in which God sees me. My eye and God's eye are one eye, one seeing, one knowing, and one loving."[2] As a result, they are leaving the familiar, much like those who left William Shakespeare's court in Act II of *As You Like It*, in search of "tongues in trees, books in running brooks, sermons in stones, and good in everything."[3] They want unity.

However, as we examine this desire for unity within the context of a shared humanity as well as within the context of a common divinity, we see, fundamentally, a core reason why we are witnessing a growing divide between the "traditionally religious" and those identifying as "spiritual but not religious."[4] Both groups tend to be quite comfortable considering the unity of our common humanity across faith traditions. However, it is when considering the unity of a common divinity that there is often a parting of the ways. Let's take a closer look at this divide.

We discover unity in our common humanity as we study the lives of key prophetic figures across traditions, finding ourselves again and again. We hear in the echoes of the past into the present the struggles, doubts, and fears as well as the triumphs, joys, and grace that inform our lives today. We recognize the deep longing that propelled each of them to answer the call, and we recognize it as our own. For example, let's look at Moses from the Hebrew Bible, Arjuna from the Hindu Bhagavad Gita, Mother Teresa representing the biblical New Testament, and Muhammad from the Qur'an.

2. McGinn, *Mystical Thought*, 149.
3. Shakespeare, *As You Like It*, 17.
4. Murphy, "Emergence of Evolutionary Panentheism," 191.

A Cry for Unity

In the Hebrew Bible, we can greatly identify with Moses when he is asked by God in Exod 3:10 to go before Pharaoh "to bring my people, the Israelites, out of Egypt." You want me to do *what?* Though biblical scholars do not agree on exactly what it is, it appears Moses has some kind of speech impediment as he argues in Exod 4:10, "I am slow of speech and slow of tongue."[5] He is likely afraid he will embarrass both himself and God and so he strongly resists as we see in Exod 3:11, "Who am I that I should go to Pharaoh, and bring the Israelites out of Egypt?"

Who am I? Is this not a question we too ask when confronted with some task we know is going to challenge us greatly? Momentarily, Moses has forgotten that he is not alone in his challenge. Indeed, God assures him in Exod 4:12, "Now go, and I will be with your mouth and teach you what you are to speak." How blessed to know that we, too, are not alone, that the Lord walks with us into our greatest fears, transforming them and us.

We know the torment of Arjuna, the great warrior in the Hindu allegory the Bhagavad Gita. Arjuna has been called to lead the forces of goodness against the forces of evil to right a wrong and restore justice. Yet at the critical moment he folds and is unable to rise up and do his duty. Seeing those he knows and respects along with the unjust across the battlefield, he is being charged to confront the enemies *within* in order to see and respond appropriately *without*.

And so are we. If we suspect wrongdoing in our work place, do we speak up? If we suspect that counseling will help a divisive or hurtful pattern within our family, do we seek help? If not, Krishna is not sympathetic. His response to Arjuna in 2:2–3: "From whence arises this shameful and cowardly dejection, Arjuna, which at this dangerous moment bars the way to heaven? Stand up, Scorcher of foes, wake up!"[6] And we too realize we miss the doorway to heaven when we do not rise up to face the truth before, and within, us.

We can imagine what was arising in the heart of Mother Teresa when she received her "call within a call" in 1946 while on a

---

5. Coogan, *New Oxford Annotated Bible*, 88n.
6. Satchidananda, *Living Gita*, 10.

train going to her annual retreat in Darjeeling.[7] The call instructed her to leave the Sisters of Loreto and establish a new order, the Missionaries of Charity, to work in the slums with the poorest of the poor.[8] In addition to this new directive, she also had to face the great doubts of many around her. One archbishop said, "I knew Mother Teresa when she was a novice and she couldn't even light the candles. And you want to make her head of a congregation? She's not able to do that."[9] And her mother superior for twenty years said, "Every day we met with Mother Teresa. We met for prayers, for meals, for recreation. I saw nothing special about her. She was just like the rest of us. We all thought she was a bit on the delicate side."[10]

How often are we, too, confronted with the opinions of those around us and with how challenging it can be when those opinions do not support our deepest callings? Still, she responded to God's inner call, and, "without even a plan, she went to the poor."[11] With faith and trust, we are reminded we don't have to have it all figured out and that, perhaps, it is our job to concentrate on the *what* and let God take care of the *how*.

Finally, we can relate to Muhammad, who called himself "God's Standing Miracle"[12] because he had no explanation as to why God would choose him, someone unschooled and barely able to write his name, through whom to bring forth the Qur'an. One day, while Muhammad was praying in a cave of a mountain on the outskirts of Mecca, known as Mount Hira, an angel appeared instructing him three times to "Proclaim!" and each time Muhammad protested, "I am not a proclaimer." Finally, the angel charged Muhammad, "Proclaim in the name of your Lord who created man from a clot of blood. Proclaim: your Lord is the Most Generous who teaches by the pen—teaches man what he knew not"

7. Royal and Woods, *Mother Teresa*, 21.
8. Royal and Woods, *Mother Teresa*, 21.
9. *Mother Teresa*, Petrie and Petrie, DVD.
10. *Mother Teresa*, Petrie and Petrie, DVD.
11. *Mother Teresa*, Petrie and Petrie, DVD.
12. Smith, *World's Religions*, 231.

(Qur'an 96:1–3).[13] Terrified, Muhammad fled home to confess to his wife Khadija that he had either become a prophet or was "one possessed—mad."[14]

In the personal caves of our own prayer lives, we too can relate to the spiritual anguish that often arises when we feel we have been called to a task for which we do not feel prepared or suited. Was that really the voice of God? Can I trust what I just heard? Yet over the next twenty-three years, God would reveal the Qur'an to Muhammad.[15] Muhammad's example challenges each of us to become a "standing miracle" in response to God's call, to be the instrument of his choosing, to that which may be beyond our understanding.

Being able to find our self within the spiritual journeys of Moses, Arjuna, Mother Teresa, and Muhammad begins to open a door to the common ground of our humanity across faith traditions. We can imagine our fellow Jewish, Hindu, Christian, and Muslim brothers and sisters engaging the same human questions, struggles as well as victories, as we do. Perhaps we can even begin to look beyond the outer differences to better see the face of our neighbor everywhere and, in time, understand ever more deeply the possibility of Jesus's command that we *love* our neighbor as our self. As Hadewijch expressed, "The madness of love is a blessed fate. It brings into unity what was divided. It makes the stranger a neighbor, and what was lowly it raises on high."[16]

Yet while both the "traditionally religious" and the "spiritual but not religious" can appreciate the quest for unity of our common humanity across faith traditions, to approach a divine unity, it turns out, is an entirely different matter. Even the Parliament of World Religions, at the 2015 Conference, supported a theme, in part, focusing on celebrating difference instead of seeking a common theology uniting all faiths.[17] And many interfaith lead-

---

13. Smith, *World's Religions*, 225–26.
14. Smith, *World's Religions*, 226.
15. Smith, *World's Religions*, 232.
16. Hooper, *Hymns to the Beloved*, 179.
17. Kwiecien, "Report," lecture.

ers stress relating to those of other faith traditions from the deep roots of one's own tradition. Appreciate one another but leave one another's God alone. We are encouraged to enjoy our common humanity, encouraged to work for a sense of unity and peace with all, but to stay clear of any notion of a common divinity across faith traditions.

However, I believe the "spiritual but not religious" are searching for a divine unity unbound from the constraints they perceive are imposed by existing faith traditions. And as more and more seekers are exploring across faith traditions, more are becoming aware of the commonalities related to our personal spiritual quests, human *and* divine, past *and* present.

Serious and thoughtful questions arise from both sides. The religious traditionalist may wonder and, indeed, fear that seeking common unifying elements may erode the long-held importance and influence of specific revelation arising from particular traditions. They may, rightly so, sound the alarm signaling the dangers of exporting or overlaying practices, thereby erasing the distinct experiences of others. And the "spiritual but not religious" seeker, exploring across faith traditions, may begin to, unexpectedly, struggle to identify an unnamed God displaced from any historical tradition of story, belief, and practice. How *do* I go about articulating a theology that resonates with my experience? What *do* I believe?

Yet, recalling Tagore's quote from the introduction, as we set our sails, a new day is appearing on the horizon bringing an opportunity to reframe this existing tension. I would argue we do *not* have to choose between the depth found within the long study of a particular faith tradition and the ubiquitous experience of the divine across traditions. In fact, I would argue that, in this age of change, we are being asked to affirm that *both* are possible. Does a Christian practicing contemplative prayer need to chant a *wazifa* practice from the Qur'an to expand spiritual understanding? Does a Hindu engaging in mantra meditation need to study the Torah to optimize awareness? Indeed, not. And yet, those who have tasted practices across traditions, as I, report having found themselves tuned to sing those "songs of Love" to God—as exalted in the quote opening the introduction—again and again.

As an interfaith theologian, I am in constant search of that which unites the world's faith traditions while, simultaneously, seeking to respect, indeed celebrate, what differentiates. It has been my observation that religious *beliefs* tend to differentiate while religious *experience* tends to engender resonance. Entering into the sound of God through the *Sonic Trilogy of Love*, practitioners from differing faith traditions can circumvent the quagmire of divisive dialogue that often occurs around beliefs. Each tradition retains its depth and beauty undiluted by any generic distilling. Traditionally religious practitioners continue to feel those reverberations of the sound of God emanating from their sacred texts as, perhaps, they have long experienced. And practitioners identifying as "spiritual but not religious" can also experience the sound of God, only now emanating from the sacred texts and practices across faith traditions.

As both "traditionally religious" and "spiritual but not religious" *Lovers,* practitioners, enter into the *Love,* sacred sound, the conditions are set for unforeseen moments of mystical unity with their *Beloved,* God. The rich historical tapestry of religious tradition is preserved even as the *Sonic Trilogy of Love* points all practitioners in the direction of the universality of the *experience* of God. Within the *Sonic Trilogy of Love*, both the "traditionally religious" and "spiritual but not religious" can find a home as each discovers, as the Greek philosopher Empedocles, "The nature of God is a circle of which the center is everywhere and the circumference is nowhere."[18]

---

18. Knowles, *Oxford Dictionary of Quotations,* 19.

2

Harmonic Preludes

How do I talk to a little flower?
Through it I talk to the Infinite. And what is the Infinite?
It is that still small voice that calls up the fairies.
Dr. George Washington Carver[1]

It is right in front of us. Just like the flower Dr. George Washington Carver always wore in the buttonhole of his jacket. Born into slavery, this renowned botanist, scientist, and inventor of the late nineteenth century did not know his birthday. He did not know his birth name. Yet he knew well *that still small voice.* "All my life I have risen regularly at four o'clock and have gone into the woods and talked with God. There He gives me my orders for the day."[2] Such orders would result in three hundred new uses for the peanut and one hundred and fifty new uses for the sweet potato as well as in the rebuilding of the entire agricultural South.[3]

1. Clark, *Man Who Talks.*
2. Clark, *Man Who Talks,* 21.
3. Clark, *Man Who Talks,* 11.

His life and works, I believe, largely encapsulate the current quest to know that which is right in front of us. The "spiritual but not religious" seekers, on their quest for God, yearn for just such a taste of the mystical and, yet, as with Dr. Carver, a mystical that informs everyday life—and, in particular, their life. They too would like to make contact with *that still small voice*, experience unity with all, and become instruments in service to a greater good.

Engaging the *Sonic Trilogy of Love*, seekers may, indeed, encounter *that still small voice* by engaging those very sacred sound practices embedded in the ancient religious canons. For in doing so, the transformational effects of sacred sound open a portal into an unmitigated experience of the divine. Here, we, the practitioner, as *Lover*, enter into the sacred sounds of the ancient canons, the *Love*, thereby creating the conditions to experience unity with the divine, the *Beloved*. I call it a crucible of transcendence, for in such moments of unity we can no longer distinguish separation between us as the *Lover* and our *Beloved*, God. Love as the core organizing principle unifies *Lover*, *Love*, and *Beloved* alike as it constantly circles in on itself. Now, we can relate to what St. Catherine of Genoa expressed: "My Me is God, nor do I recognize any other Me except my God Himself."[4] In such moments of unity, we are touched by the mystical, that which is beyond our understanding yet, now, is more real to us than what we may have previously thought.

As we emerge from the *Sonic Trilogy of Love*, the remembrance of this unity begins to imprint our daily walk. More often, we sense that God does not so much live in us as we live in God, as St. Therese of Lisieux declared, "I am the atom of Jesus,"[5] and the Indian mystic Kabir expressed, "All know that the drop merges into the ocean, but few know that the ocean merges into the drop."[6] And with this profound awareness, we find our heart and God's heart, more often, pulsing together. Though keenly aware of our particularity, we now start to see the face of God everywhere—in

---

4. Huxley, *Perennial Philosophy*, 11.
5. Therese of Lisieux, *Poetry*, 106.
6. Kabir, *Bijak*, 96.

our neighbor and in the flower. This is how the *Love* has its way with us, transforming us and leaving us not where we began—in unity with all.

And in quiet moments, we hear echoes of St. Anselm: "Let me seek thee in longing, let me long for thee in seeking: let me find Thee in love and love Thee in finding."[7] Notice that in relation to love, *thee* is capitalized. This is because love could be called the fundamental essence of divine consciousness, a consciousness that speaks to us in its own language, opening us to what was closed to heal our deepest wounds, shape our unique purpose, sound our glorious, unchecked, ecstatic cry, and, ultimately, to answer our deepest longing by uniting us to him, to *Love*, to all.

Great mystics, theologians and philosophers have experienced this ecstatic state across the ages. For example, in *Echoes from Perennial Philosophy*, we recognize the theological underpinnings of this new paradigm, the *Sonic Trilogy of Love*, most notably emanating from the works of Aldous Huxley, Friedrich Schleiermacher, and William James. Yet, we also see in *Panentheism: Emerging Philosophical Worldview* how the *Trilogy* is an excellent paradigm for today offering seekers an intimate, unmitigated, experience of the divine. Let's take a look at both past and present.

Echoes from Perennial Philosophy

English philosopher and writer Aldous Huxley describes perennial philosophy as being "primarily concerned with the one divine Reality substantial to the manifold world of things and lives and minds."[8] Critical to the formation of the *Sonic Trilogy of Love* is Aldous Huxley's assertion that, "Rudiments of the Perennial Philosophy may be found among the traditional lore of primitive peoples in every region of the world, and in its fully developed forms has a place in every one of the higher religions."[9]

7. Huxley, *Perennial Philosophy*, 224.
8. Huxley, *Perennial Philosophy*, viii.
9. Huxley, *Perennial Philosophy*, vii.

HARMONIC PRELUDES

If we listen closely we can hear the one divine Reality speaking through many of the world's faith traditions. We hear it echoed by the Psalmist, "Where can I go from your spirit? Or where can I flee from your presence?" (Ps 139:7) and recorded by early kabbalist Moshe Cordovero: "The essence of divinity is found in every single thing—nothing but it exists (Shiur Qomah to Zohar 3:14b, Idra Rabba)."[10] It was exclaimed by Meister Eckhart: "To gauge the soul we must gauge it with God, for the Ground of God and the Ground of the Soul are one and the same... The knower and the known are one."[11] In the Dao, it is called Principle: "Do not ask whether the Principle is in this or in that; it is in all beings... It has ordained that all things should be limited, but is Itself unlimited, infinite."[12] The great Sufi poet Jalaluddin Rumi called it Beloved: "The Beloved is all in all; the lover merely veils Him; The Beloved is all that lives, the lover a dead thing."[13] And in Buddhism it is garnered as, "One Nature... the Tathagata-garbha, (literally, Buddha-womb)," where "One Reality, all comprehensive, contains within itself all realities."[14]

Yet it is in the historical roots of Hinduism where, Huxley asserts, we find the most succinct expression of this one divine Reality expressed in the Sanskrit formula *tat tvam asi*, "That thou art." In this well-known formula, *tat* or "That" refers to God, *tvam* or "thou" to us, and *asi* or "art" to a state of being. It is the final goal of every human being to discover this fact for himself, to "know the 'That' which is 'Thou.'"[15] Along the way, the seeker realizes that God, "That," is within all peoples *and* without in all creation. As Huxley asserts, the seeker comes to realize that God is "at once the principle of his own *thou* and of all other *thous*, animate and inanimate."[16] Hence, within the *Sonic Trilogy of Love*, as we come

10. Artson, "Holy, Holy, Holy!" 29.
11. Huxley, *Perennial Philosophy*, 12.
12. Huxley, *Perennial Philosophy*, 7.
13. Huxley, *Perennial Philosophy*, 15.
14. Huxley, *Perennial Philosophy*, 8.
15. Huxley, *Perennial Philosophy*, 4.
16. Huxley, *Perennial Philosophy*, 4.

in contact with our own *thou* we begin to see how it is possible to have an experience of mystical unity with all other *thous*. And in addition, we can now better understand how Dr. George Washington Carver came to recognize the Infinite through a flower.

Still, most traditions hold that this one divine Reality "cannot be directly and immediately apprehended except by those who have chosen to fulfill certain conditions, making themselves loving, pure in heart, and poor in spirit."[17] This is why Jesus said, "Blessed are the pure in heart, for they will see God" (Matt 5:8), and Ansari of Herat said, "Would you become a pilgrim on the road of Love? The first condition is that you make yourself humble as dust and ashes."[18]

When we as *Lovers*, practitioners, enter into the *Love*, sacred sound, in the *Sonic Trilogy of Love*, the conditions are set for an unmitigated experience of this one divine Reality, the *Beloved*, God. Yet most assuredly, in the process we are made pure of heart and humble as dust and ashes so that, in unforeseen moments, we may experience nothing between us, *tvam*, and God, *tat*. In such moments, there is no separation as we find ourselves in mystical unity with our Beloved.

And in doing so we slowly come to see the holy, the miraculous, in plain sight right in front of us. As the German philosopher and theologian Friedrich Schleiermacher writes, "'Miracle' is merely the religious name for event, everyone one of which, even the most natural and usual . . . as soon as it adapts itself to the fact that the religious view of it can be the dominate one. To me everything is a miracle."[19] And what is it that allows this religious view to become dominate? Love. In his sermon "To Love and Good Works," he explores the true essence of this love, proclaiming, "It is love that changes things transitory in themselves into something eternal and heavenly, and stamps them with her own divine impress."[20] Robert R. Williams summarized it beauti-

---

17. Huxley, *Perennial Philosophy*, viii.
18. Huxley, *Perennial Philosophy*, 88.
19. Schleiermacher, *On Religion*, 49.
20. Schleiermacher, *Selected Sermons*, 400.

fully, saying that for Schleiermacher, "Divine love is the foundation and ordering principle in the value-nucleus of the Christian God-consciousness; love is that which, and through which, all other elements—including the full eternal-omnipotence—come into positive expression."[21]

It was believing in divine love as the foundation and ordering principle of God-consciousness that led Schleiermacher to adopt this deep sense of the miraculous and the mystical in everyday life. And, as with Huxley, he described this religious view as seeing the miraculous in the animate and well as in the inanimate. Simply, Schleiermacher truly had "a strong sense of the organic whole of things."[22] Now, from this view, we too may begin to see the flower in a way we may have missed before. Moreover, Schleiermacher believed that such moments of mysticism could not be completely comprehended leading him to describe those who had experienced such as being "seers of the Infinite."[23]

In the *Sonic Trilogy of Love*, the *Lover*, practitioner, through engaging *Love*, the sacred sound of God, may, indeed, experience the dominance of this religious view and, in such moments, unexpectedly, become a seer of the infinite, seeing into the whole of things and finding only the miraculous, the *Beloved*, God.

Lastly, in addition to Aldous Huxley and Friedrich Schleiermacher, I include American philosopher and psychologist William James among those perennial philosophers whose work has contributed to the theological underpinnings of the *Sonic Trilogy of Love*. James's well-known pragmatism accentuated not only the study of religious experience but the practical consequences of such experience observable in daily life. As he asserts, "To determine the meaning of the idea of God and to bring out the real differences in the debate, one ought to consider actual religious experiences and the practical consequences for people's lives."[24] Dr. Carver would have concurred, as he was able to offer humankind

21. Williams, *Schleiermacher the Theologian*, 127.
22. Chapman, *Introduction to Schleiermacher*, 107.
23. Chapman, *Introduction to Schleiermacher*, 139.
24. Proudfoot, *William James*, 2.

the practical consequence of many new uses for the peanut and the sweet potato.

Indeed, in his well-known *The Varieties of Religious Experience*, James proposed that traditional philosophy of religion be replaced by a "science of religions" to study religious beliefs, experiences, and practices, whereby even the most private, mystical experiences offered as evidence for religious belief could be brought out into the open for public scrutiny and evaluation. As James writes, "I do not see why a critical Science of Religions of this sort might not eventually command as general a public adhesion as is commanded by a physical science."[25]

While ever the pragmatist, James held a theological view similar to Huxley's and Schleiermacher's, one that included an emphasis on mysticism, which he claimed to be the "root and center of all religion."[26] In addition, he observed that each individual was fully capable of identifying his being with "the germinal higher part of himself."[27] Indeed, James reported that, common to the experiences he had studied, there was within an individual's consciousness this "higher part conterminous and continuous with a 'more' of the same quality, which is operative in the universe outside of him, and which he can keep in working touch with."[28]

And we too, as *Lovers* entering into the *Sonic Trilogy of Love*, may, through the *Love*, sacred sound, come in contact with that germinal higher part of ourselves, that something "more," our *Beloved*, God. And, graciously, as a result of our newly found awareness within, we may start to experience our own unique practical consequences without manifesting in daily life in service to a greater good.

Yet, our discussion would not be complete without giving voice to some of the key criticisms of perennial philosophy. A common criticism is reported to be its tendency to inadequately address the problem of pain and suffering while, simultaneously,

25. James, *Works*, 359–60.
26. Hood, "Mystical Self," 9.
27. James, *Works*, 400.
28. James, *Works*, 400.

overemphasizing the notion that all practitioners, with proper desire and discipline, may aspire to enlightenment. For example, Ronald Hope, critiquing the work of Aldous Huxley, addresses both aspects, citing what he calls the "perennial problem" leaving unresolved why pain and suffering are so unevenly distributed. And at the other end of the spectrum, he questions the assumption that, given the commitment to stringent spiritual disciplines, all peoples may become mystics should they so desire.[29]

In response to the first concern I would answer that all seekers, in varying degrees, encounter layers of long-held inner pain and suffering on their way to unity with God. Transformation within the *Sonic Trilogy of Love* denotes a deeply personal healing journey. I see no value or purpose in comparing one's suffering to that of others or to delineate a hierarchy of suffering in relation to others. To Hope's question, "Is it true that all peoples may become mystics if they want to?"[30] I would answer, "No." Certainly, when entering into the *Sonic Trilogy of Love*, conditions are set for the practitioner to experience unforeseen *moments* of unity with God. And, while these blessed moments do begin to inform daily experience, it is not usually the case that practitioners become mystics or saints—unless, in the rare occasion, such an occurrence has already been ordained by God. Most importantly, it would not be advisable for any practitioner to enter into the *Sonic Trilogy of Love* for the purpose of becoming a mystic. Rather, it is entering with a humble heart that opens the *Lover*, practitioner, to that which is beyond understanding.

Panentheism: Emerging Philosophical Worldview

As noted in the introduction, panentheism is an emerging worldview presently unfamiliar to many scholars and most

---

29. Hope, "Huxley's Philosophy," 106.
30. Hope, "Huxley's Philosophy," 106.

practitioners.[31] Yet it points to the phenomena silently thriving among the masses today, encapsulating both the shifts currently taking place in religious practice and the emerging changes and ramifications occurring as a result of the quest being instituted by the "spiritual but not religious." Particular to our purposes here, it most succinctly describes theologically what the *Sonic Trilogy of Love* offers experientially.

Different from the familiar pantheism, which holds that God and creation are one, panentheism offers a new way to think about God that affirms both immanent *and* transcendent qualities.[32] As a philosophical worldview, panentheism originated in the early nineteenth century in Friedrich Schelling's *Of Human Freedom* and was later articulated by Karl Christian Friedrich Krause in 1829. In the early twentieth century, Charles Hartshorne formulated the now classic definition of panentheism as a concept composed of five features descriptive of panentheistic divinity: God is eternal, temporal, consciousness, knowing of the world, and inclusive of the world.[33] Within the *Sonic Trilogy of Love*, practitioners, or *Lovers*, experience God's, the *Beloved's*, immanence through the *Love*, sacred sound. Yet the *Beloved* transcends any one sacred script or practice to include all.

Analysis of the Greek roots of the term fully reveals its immanent qualities as well as its transcendent potentialities. *Pan* ("all") + *en* ("in") + *theos* ("God"): all is in God.[34] One could say this is a restatement of our previous discussion highlighting that God does not so much live in us as we live in God. Marcus Borg, New Testament scholar, theologian, and author, described it this way: "God is more than everything (and thus transcendent), yet everything is in God (hence God is immanent). For Panentheism, God is 'right here,' even as God is also more than 'right here.'"[35] Christian Medieval mystic Mechthild of Magdeburg expressed the *experience* of

---

31. Clayton, "Panentheism in the Tapestry," 201.
32. Artson, "Holy, Holy, Holy!" 20.
33. Biernacki, "Panentheism Outside the Box," 3.
34. Artson, "Holy, Holy, Holy!" 20.
35. Artson, "Holy, Holy, Holy!" 20.

this immanent transcendence this way: "The day of my spiritual awakening was the day I saw, and knew I saw, God in all things and all things in God."[36] And from the Eastern faith traditions, we find panentheism embedded in what is called the *Royal Secret* that Krishna, God personified, tells Arjuna in the Bhagavad Gita: "Unmanifest, I pervade the entire universe. All creatures exist in me, yet I am not contained [exclusively] in all of them. (9:4).[37] Indeed, God is limitless far beyond the limited expressions we see.

Panentheism has profound implications both theologically and personally. As we have noted with the examples above, this heretical fusion of matter and divinity can be traced to a number of premodern expressions. However, it can also be seen as an apt description for the transitions occurring today. Loriliai Biernacki suggests in *Panentheism across World Traditions* that the "*pan* ['all'] in panentheism ought to be seen in a different sense, one that maintains the multivocality of the whole."[38] Further, she suggests that the historical reaches of the *pan* in panentheism, found in other regions and other times, "set the stage for a kind of comparative theology that can both begin to deconstruct the older models of hegemony and bridge horizons across separate worlds."[39] Therefore, she describes the currently prevailing panentheism as a kind of "antitheology" insofar as it stands in opposition to hegemonic truth claims.[40]

When considering what the bridge might be across separate worlds, panentheism, in keeping with its antitheological nature, does not go in search of a new "theism." Instead, it seeks "linking and connectivity"[41] that does not trump traditions but "ideally allows each to speak in its own voice."[42] As Jeaneane Fowler writes, "The ultimate transcendency of God never permits him to be

36. Twyan, *Proof,* 20.
37. Satchidananda, *Living Gita,* 129.
38. Biernacki, "Panentheism Outside the Box," 5.
39. Biernacki, "Panentheism Outside the Box," 5.
40. Biernacki, "Panentheism Outside the Box," 5.
41. Biernacki, "Panentheism Outside the Box," 10.
42. Clayton, "Panentheism in the Tapestry," 201.

merely the pantheistic whole that unites the parts: while causative, he panentheistically transcends all."[43] Panentheism links traditions simply with a universal acknowledgement that each has a rich heritage of God's immanence *and* transcendence that is uniquely expressed within each faith tradition. Within the *Sonic Trilogy of Love*, practitioners concretize this sacrality, linking all faiths, as they enter into the universality of the *experience* of God.

Personally, panentheism offers an opportunity to reframe the more common belief that God lives in us or may relate to us in some unique way as dictated by a particular faith tradition. We may be used to thinking of *ourselves* as instruments through which God may offer blessing, healing, grace. But does the instrument contain the song? No. It simply allows for the expression of the song. If we live in God, this begins to make sense. Now, as we release our need to have proprietary ownership of God, a certain freedom comes in simply offering ourselves up as instruments through which our *Beloved*, God, may express. And in such moments we delight in the immanence *and* are left silent and humbled by the transcendence. Mystics across faith traditions have attested to this great truth. As Jewish scholar Bradley Shavit Artson observed, "A panentheistic understanding of God recognizes the undomesticated nature of all reality and responds with awe and wonder."[44]

The second syllable in panentheism, *en*, points to this very merging of the immanence and the transcendence which we may experience personally. As professor of constructive theology, Catherine Keller writes, "That little preposition holds open the possibility not just of the symbolization of an infinity greater than the sum of its own parts as divine but also of a *relation* to that divinity." Without the *en*, she concludes, God would remain "chillingly indifferent" to us.[45] Instead, we experience a "power of mutual relation" that summons an energy "that at certain moments we name love."[46] Within the *Sonic Trilogy of Love, Lovers*, practitioners, as

---

43. Clayton, "Panentheism in the Tapestry, 202–3.
44. Artson, "Holy, Holy, Holy!" 24–25.
45. Keller, "Body of Panentheism," 64.
46. Keller, "Body of Panentheism," 66.

they enter into the *Love*, sacred sound, progressively come into full relation with the *Beloved*, God, inherent in *all* creation.

Such *Lovers* begin to realize the truth expressed in the Qur'an, al-Baqarah 2:115: "To Allah belong the east and the west: so whichever way you turn, there is the face of Allah!"[47] And they can now relate to Shug in Alice Walker's *The Color Purple* describing her journey away from an image of God as an old white man. She says first there were "trees. Then air. Then birds. Then other people." And, "Then one day," she explains, "I knew that if I cut a tree, my arm would bleed. God is everywhere."[48]

Finally, a key aspect of this emerging worldview is the convergence of "science and scientific models with a broader vision of the divine."[49] I would agree with Philip Clayton, a constructive Christian theologian, who said, "Perhaps what we call the scientific and the religious are two faces, two dimensions, of a single human quest. If that's right, the tools of science and deep spirituality of the panentheistic 'all in God' can mutually constrain each other, like yin and yang within the Dao."[50]

I would argue that, historically, our quest for God has been largely exemplified by the ancient Hindu allegory, called the *Blind Men and the Elephant*. In this tale, replicated with minor revisions across many faith traditions, blind men come together to learn about an elephant, yet each man only touches one part. Afterwards, they compare notes and find themselves in total disagreement. The lesson is, of course, that no one blind man has a complete experience of the elephant, though each believes that his part contains the full knowledge of the elephant. Perhaps science, philosophy, religion, and so on are each like the blind men, each having acquired intimate knowledge of their part of the elephant, or of universal Truth, yet, historically, having mistakenly believed that they have held the whole Truth.

---

47. Qara'i, *Qur'un*, 25.
48. Baker-Fletcher, *Dancing with God*, 66.
49. Biernacki, "Panentheism Outside the Box," 8.
50. Clayton, "Panentheism in the Tapestry," 210.

But now, we are in an age when though "once blind we now may see," to reference the well-known hymn "Amazing Grace," traces of the whole elephant coming into focus right before us. For example, in 2011, at the University of Colorado in Boulder, Catholic monk Ernesto Cardenal read aloud his poetry, "suffused with the substance of science, quoting physics throughout, lyrical reflections on the Big Bang and evolution and myriad galaxies." Following his talk, in answer to a question about faith in God, he declared, "God has the capacity to be both present here, immanent in this fragile world, and at the same time transcendent, beyond what we beings in bodies on our small globe can imagine."[51] Panentheism.

The life and works of Dr. George Washington Carver effortlessly embodied a synthesis of science and religion. He boldly invited us to *see* the whole, the Truth, right before us, to *see* the flower, immanent *and* Infinite. This experience of the mystical, I would argue, is exactly the destination the "spiritual but not religious" are seeking on their quest for God.

Yet, as in our discussion of perennial philosophy, it is important to note differing voices, many deeply religious, offering another response to this emerging panentheistic worldview. In "A Postconservative Evangelical Response to Panentheism," Roger E. Olson states that evangelicals have largely rejected panentheism, as in their view, "it implies a dependence of God on the World."[52] They, instead, tend to largely concur with Baptist theologian Augustus Hopkins Strong that "the universe is not self-existent or eternal; it began to be a certain number of years ago. And it has its origin, as it has its subsistence from hour to hour, in the power and will of One who is as much above it as the thinker is above his thoughts or the agent above his acts."[53] Like many conservative evangelicals, he categorically rejects the idea of the world being "in God" or any position implying or asserting a dependency of God on the world.

51. Biernacki, "Panentheism Outside the Box," 8.
52. Olsen, "Response to Panentheism," 332.
53. Olsen, "Response to Panentheism," 333.

Clearly, the opposing point of view arises from the fundamental ontological difference in conceptualizing *what God is*. Panentheistically, God is believed to immanently pervade all creation as well as to transcend creation. The conservative Christian evangelical perspective would hold that God is separate from his creation and, therefore, able to exercise voluntary choice over involvement. Yet, interestingly, it should be noted that *Lovers,* or practitioners, experiencing moments of transcendence within the *Sonic Trilogy of Love,* often discover a God that is simultaneously universal and omnipresent as well as deeply personal and relational.

Critical to our discussion here is that whether one believes that such an experience is bestowed by God voluntarily or that it occurs panentheistically through God's immanent and transcendent qualities does not influence, nor negate, the unifying experience. It is precisely for this reason that Christian evangelicals and persons holding a panentheistic view, as well as both the "traditionally religious" and the "spiritual but not religious," all can find unity with God within the *Sonic Trilogy of Love.*

Now, in part 2, "Answering the Call: *The Sonic Trilogy of Love,*" we are ready to examine this new paradigm in depth, first distilling its structural elements making it a suitable crucible for transcendence, and then exploring its components: *Lover, Love* and *Beloved* in the journey to mystical unity where all falls away except God.

PART 2

Answering the Call
The Sonic Trilogy of Love

3

The Crucible of Transcendence

I was a hidden treasure and yearned to be known.
Therefore, I created the creatures so that I might be known.
HADITH QUDSI: IBN AL-'ARABI[1]

IT IS OUR DEEP desire, longing, to be united with our God that ignites us to answer the call of the mourning dove and brings us to the crucible of transcendence, the *Sonic Trilogy of Love*. Here, as *Lovers*, we engage the sonic aspect of the divine, the *Love*, creating the conditions to experience mystical moments of unity with our *Beloved*. And for most practitioners, these are just moments—yet moments that leave us not where we began. Here we encounter just a glimpse of that *hidden treasure* as our *Beloved* makes himself known to us. Entering into the *Sonic Trilogy of Love*, we are acutely aware of our unique particularity. Yet through the portal of sacred sound, we are poised to lose ourselves and experience a unity, as yet, unknown to us. And in such moments, we experience what St. Dionysius described by saying, "God is a fountain flowing

---

1. Chittick, *The Sufi Path of Knowledge.*

into itself,"[2] for we can no longer distinguish between us and our *Beloved*. The treasure we have long pursued we find was within us all along. As Jesus reminded us, "Nor will they say, 'Look, here it is!' or 'There it is!' For, in fact, the kingdom of God is within you" (Luke 17:21).

Before entering into the *Sonic Trilogy of Love*, let's take a closer look at this sacred crucible of transcendence. Here we find three key aspects necessary to our overall understanding: the structure and power of the trifold paradigm detailed in *The Root of Perfection: The Number 3*; a clear definition of *love* as it is used in this context in *Love Defined*; and, the importance of silence in relation to sacred sound in *The Role of Silence*.

The Root of Perfection: The Number 3

Why a *Trilogy*? Exploring the mystical theology of the Eastern Orthodox Church, we find a clue. St. Gregory Nazianzen, when reflecting upon the Christian Trinity, expressed it this way: "Two is a number which separates, three the number which transcends all separation: the one and the many find themselves gathered and circumscribed in the Trinity."[3] Describing the number three as one that unifies, he states,

> No sooner do I conceive of the One than I am illuminated by the splendor of the Three; no sooner do I distinguish them than I am carried back to the One. When I think of any One of the Three, I think of Him as a whole, and my eyes are filled, and the greater part of what I am thinking of escapes me. I cannot grasp the greatness of that One so as to attribute a greater greatness to the rest. When I contemplate the Three together, I see but one torch, and cannot divide or measure out the undivided light.[4]

---

2. Linge, "Mysticism," 474.
3. Lossky, *Mystical Theology*, 47.
4. Lossky, *Mystical Theology*, 46.

The Crucible of Transcendence

The Greek fathers always maintained that the principle of unity in the Trinity was "the person of the Father."[5] In this light, the "threefold number was not, as we commonly understand it, a quantity."[6] Indeed, it expresses a united hypostasis, whereby the sum is always unity, 3 = 1. "It expresses the ineffable order within the Godhead."[7] Panentheistically, we experience the *Beloved's immanence* through the *Love*, sacred sound, yet our *Beloved* also remains the ineffable *transcendent*, equally responsive to practitioners across faith traditions.

In the early Christian Church, St. Augustine also referenced this triune: "Behold, when I who seek this love, this involves three things: I, that which I love and love itself. Therefore, there are three: a person who loves, that which is loved, and love."[8] In similar fashion to the Eastern Church, St. Augustine, discussing the single divine nature equally possessed by all three persons of the Trinity, writes in his *De Trinitate*, "Therefore, the Father is omnipotent, the Son omnipotent and the Holy Spirit omnipotent; yet, there are not three omnipotents, but one omnipotent, 'from whom all things, through whom all things, in whom all things' (Rom 11:36)."[9] Today, the Reverend Dr. Carter Heyward, a feminist liberation theologian and a leading voice among lesbian, gay, bisexual, and transgender Christians, has affirmed this relational aspect of this omnipotent Father, Son, and Holy Spirit in her Relational Trinity: "God as Lover, Beloved, [and] Spirit of Love" declaring that it is the Spirit of Love that binds the Lover to her Beloved.[10]

In the *Sonic Trilogy of Love*, it is, indeed, the Spirit of Love, here expressed through the *Love* as sacred sound, that unites us as *Lovers* to our *Beloved*. And in such moments, we do, blessedly, experience the omnipresence, as now we are no longer distinguishable in particularity, for the relational *Love* is all that remains,

---

5. Lossky, *Mystical Theology*, 58.
6. Lossky, *Mystical Theology*, 48.
7. Lossky, *Mystical Theology*, 48.
8. Augustine, *Trinitarian Controversy*, 128.
9. Cousins, "Trinity and World Religions," 489–90.
10. Moody, *Women Encounter God*, 34.

indeed, is all that ever was or shall be. And we come to experience intimately what St. Augustine meant when he said, "Our hearts are restless until they come to rest in you."[11]

Yet this trifold paradigm of the Trinity, integral to the Christian faith, can also be found in comparable paradigms across faith traditions. In Judaism, we find this trifold paradigm in the Yesodei ha-Torah. As Maimonides points out in his great Code of Jewish Law, "God is the knower, the subject of knowledge, and the knowing itself (Yesodei ha-Torah, 2:10)."[12] Expanding on this insight, he writes, "God is the life, the living, and the source of God's own life."[13] And of this omnipresent God the Jewish tradition affirms that God is not just being but *becoming*. And so are we. Indeed, as Rabbi Bradley Shavit Artson writes, "Jewish tradition affirms the self-creating nature of creation as a gift of God. We are all of us located not in some distilled ideal of being but in the dynamic unfolding of becoming."[14]

Practitioners discover with the *Sonic Trilogy of Love* that *our becoming known to our Beloved*, God, is an ever-unfolding process as we excavate the inner treasure within ourselves. Yet, graciously, though it may feel as though God remains partly hidden from us, we learn from Jer 23:23–24 that we cannot hide from God. "Am I a God nearby, says the Lord, and not a God far off? Who can hide in secret places so that I cannot see them? says the Lord. Do I not fill heaven and earth? says the Lord."

Panentheistically, Judaism refers to the world as God's *levush*, "garment." Or, in the words of kabbalist Moshe Cordovero:

> The essence of divinity is found in every single thing—nothing but it exists. It causes every living thing to be. It enlivens them: its existence exists in each existent. Do not attribute duality to God. Realize that Ein Sof [aspect of the divine that is eternal and beyond comprehension] exists in each existent. Do not say, "This is a stone and

---

11. Augustine, *Confessions*, trans. Chadwick, 3.
12. Artson, "Holy, Holy, Holy!" 25.
13. Artson, "Holy, Holy, Holy!" 25.
14. Artson, "Holy, Holy, Holy!" 26–27.

not God." God forbid! Rather, all existence is God, and the stone is a thing pervaded by divinity.[15]

Within the *Sonic Trilogy of Love*, as we discover the hidden treasure, *Beloved*, the Ein Sof, enlivening us, suddenly, we start to recognize that same *Beloved*, Ein Sof, everywhere we look—enlivening the stones of the earth and the face of our neighbor. We know now that God is, at once, immanent and transcendent throughout all creation.

In Sufism we find this triune expressed in metaphysician Ibn al-'Arabi's "unity of being," within which he relates the practitioner's experience of the ninety-nine beautiful names of Allah: "We cannot describe him by any quality unless we are that quality. When we know him in ourselves and through ourselves we attribute to him everything we attribute to ourselves."[16] He goes on to stress that through the divine sayings, "He [Allah] described himself to us, through us. When we witness him, we witness ourselves. When we witness ourselves, we witness him."[17] As we, the *Lovers*, take in the *Love*, the sacred sound of the ninety-nine beautiful names of Allah, we are joined with our *Beloved*, Allah.

Another expression of this unity of *Lover* and *Beloved* is found in the Qur'anic principle of *tawhid*, "the unity of God, of humanity, of the universe, and of truth itself. *Tawhid* is all-Oneness, the Whole before and after existence, thus the One who transcends all duality and plurality and yet is the creator of all duality and plurality."[18] We, as *Lovers*, approach God, Allah the *Beloved*, through the conscious cultivation of God's qualities. In doing so, we find we actively surrender "to mirror God and to become a channel for God's creative expression."[19] Through the sacred sound of the ninety-nine beautiful names of Allah, we enter into the *Love*, the portal to the *tawhid*, and experience Allah, the *Beloved*.

15. Artson, "Holy, Holy, Holy!" 29.
16. Sharify-Funk and Dickson, "Traces of Panentheism," 156–57.
17. Sharify-Funk and Dickson, "Traces of Panentheism," 157.
18. Sharify-Funk and Dickson, "Traces of Panentheism," 148.
19. Sharify-Funk and Dickson, "Traces of Panentheism," 149.

Finally, from Hinduism, in the Bhagavad Gita 18:18, we find, "There are three incitements to knowledge: knowledge, what is to be known, and the knower."[20] Sri Swami Satchidananda writes in The Living Gita: The Complete Bhagavad and Commentary, "The seed of all that has manifested is in this trinity: the knowledge, the knowable and the Knower."[21] Notice he capitalizes "Knower" denoting the *Beloved*. He writes, "These three—subject, object, and the interaction within them always come up together."[22]

An understanding of this grammatical aspect of the trinity—subject, interaction (verb), and object—opens a way to understanding the difference between the finite body-mind and the infinite soul. The finite body-mind normally functions as the subject observing the everyday world as object. Yet in meditation, the thoughts, feelings and sensations of the body-mind suddenly become the objects of observation witnessed by the infinite soul. The infinite soul or "Knower," *Beloved*, on the other hand, can only function as the subject, as it is *who we are*. This distinction is an important starting place for receiving the full realization of *tat tvam asi*, "That thou art," discussed in chapter 2.

Love Defined

St. Augustine in *Homilies on the First Epistle of John* affirms clearly in the Seventh Homily on 1 John 4:4–12 that God is love and warns, "See now, that to act contrary to love is to act contrary to God."[23] But what is this love to which he is referring? I would argue that love as the core organizing principle within the *Sonic Trilogy of Love* is inherently a *devotional* love as opposed to the more conventional definition denoting love as an *emotional* experience. Devotional love stems from equanimity and is an expression of Truth. Its actions are responsive as opposed to being reactive, based on

---

20. Satchidananda, *Living Gita*, 266.
21. Satchidananda, *Living Gita*, 267.
22. Satchidananda, *Living Gita*, 267.
23. Augustine, "Inquiring after God," 213.

an emotive moment. It cannot be swayed by self-driven desire, nor can it be avoided by diversionary tactics. It is complete unto itself.

Yet this quality of love often does not denote the easy path. Practical real-world examples show why. A mother may suddenly *see* her daughter's eating disorder and know it is time for treatment. A man may awaken to another day, not remembering the night before, and know it is time to confront his addiction. It may be an employee who knows she can no longer remain silent in response to unwanted advances. It is the teen who searches for the courage to come out and claim his sexual identity. Or it may be a couple who know they must speak what has long gone silent in order to possibly find one another again. Yet, blessedly, when we have the courage to allow devotional love to have its way with us, we discover the full breath of Jesus's words, "and you will know the truth, and the truth will make you free" (John 8:32).

Within the *Sonic Trilogy of Love*, this devotional love is cultivated within the *Lover*, the practitioner, through the meditative toning of the ancient sacred sounds inherent within the spiritual practices across faith traditions. As with any practice of meditation, the intention is to give the mind a point of focus, in this case a sacred sound or mantra, in order to hone, or train, the mind to rest in equanimity. Cultivating mindful equanimity within, over time, produces more expressions of devotional love without. As the mind becomes more familiar with this state of devotional equanimity, we, as practitioners, begin to notice changes in our everyday lives reflecting what is being cultivated through daily practice. The mind slowly becomes less susceptible to the emotional highs and lows from which our reactions occur and, instead, more often responds from devotional, peaceful clarity.

Carter Heyward, mentioned earlier, describes devotional love quite succinctly in *The Redemption of God: A Theology of Mutual Relation*, when she writes, "Love is justice. It is not necessarily a happy feeling or a romantic attachment. Love is a way of being in the world, not necessarily an emotional affect."[24] She

---

24. Heyward, *Redemption of God*, 17.

goes on to say that because love has become a "catch-all for sweet and happy feelings," as well as "trivialized so thoroughly, and perverted—turned completely around—from its Gospel meaning, we find ourselves having to begin again to re-experience, re-consider, re-conceptualize what it means—to say 'I love you.'"[25] We too find that to truly love ourselves or one another, we must reexamine what we once may have thought.

Ultimately, we, the practitioner, discover that the emotion of love, often associated with happy excitement, inevitably fades as our psyche more often rests in devotional equanimity. We know now that if we need happy, its opposite, sad, soon follows. Devotional love needs nothing, seeks nothing. It becomes the anchor, the quiet inner smile, sustaining the happy as well as challenging times. I can imagine it was what sustained Mother Mary at the foot of the cross watching her beloved son Jesus be crucified. And it was the courage that enabled Arjuna to rise up and do his duty on the battlefield of life in order to overcome wrongdoing and restore justice. But sadly, many seek the emotion of love and, in doing so, miss the narrow gate that leads to life (see Matt 7:14). It's why St. John of the Cross reflected, "The imperfect [ones] destroy true devotion because they seek sensible sweetness in prayer."[26]

The Role of Silence

Rumi said, "There is a place where words are born of silence, a place where the whispers of the heart arise. There is a place where voices sing your beauty, a place where every breath carves your image in my soul."[27] And so we discover that beyond all we may have thought we desired, beyond the raging of our deepest fears, beyond all we may have long believed, perceived, or understood, the unforeseen whisper of our *Beloved* has been patiently awaiting our arrival, our emptiness, so as to carve ever more deeply those

---

25. Heyward, *Redemption of God*, 218.
26. Huxley, *Perennial Philosophy*, 255.
27. Rumi, *In the Arms*, 25.

songs of beauty into our soul. Having honed our mind into a state of equanimity, we can hear them now as silence bursts into song and we discover the full paradox of the spiritual awakening.

For now, in silence, if only for an instant, we may, unexpectedly, lose our self to find our Self as we discover again and again what the unknown author of the fourteenth-century *The Cloud of Unknowing* described: "The work of love is the total forgetfulness of self."[28] Where we may have most feared to tread, we find, mercifully, as in Ps 23, the Lord, our Shepherd, leading us into the full realization of *lo echsar*, commonly translated as we "shall not want," yet more succinctly is translated as we will "lack not."[29] Through this subtle yet critically important nuance in meaning, we discover not just that we could never be alone but, blessedly, that we are already full. We have experienced now the "single, epiphanic, truth fully apprehended only in silence."[30] And in just such a single moment, we know now, as did Meister Eckhart, that "the core of God is also my core, and the core of my soul the core of God's."[31]

It is in the silence that we uncover our *Beloved*, the hidden treasure yearning to be known through us. It is here that we begin to witness that we are the instrument, as St. Francis of Assisi described in his well-known prayer, "Lord, Make Me a Channel of Thy Peace,"[32] simply and graciously allowing the song of God to be played through us. We know now that it is our job to keep ourselves tuned in readiness so as to be available to be played in service to some greater good of which we are only a part. We understand now Hildegard of Bingen's song expressing the effects of such encounters with unity: "Love overflows into all things, from out of the depths to above the highest stars."[33]

---

28. McGinn, "English Mystics," 200.
29. Scherman and Zlotwitz, *Tehillim*, 56.
30. Beck, *Sonic Theology*, 79.
31. Linge, "Mysticism," 477.
32. Vardey, *Mother Teresa*, 181–82.
33. Young, "Holy Women," 406.

The Call of the Mourning Dove

So we keep returning to the crucible of transcendence. We keep submitting to daily practice. We keep engaging the *Love*, sacred sound, to create the conditions within which our *Beloved* inner treasure may graciously become known to us and through us.

4

Lover: Practitioner

Deep in the hearts of all, there is the light of all lights forever beyond darkness.

BHAGAVAD GITA[1]

AND SO, WE HEAR the call of the mourning dove and like an excited, expectant bride, we respond. We may have a long way to go before we enter into a "spiritual marriage"[2] with our Beloved, as St. Teresa of Ávila describes in the seventh dwelling place of the interior castle, the symbol she used to explain the interior journey to God. But like Teresa, we too yearn to journey deep within to touch our soul, that "single diamond," shining bright like a "very clear crystal,"[3] much like that *light of all lights forever beyond darkness* from the Bhagavad Gita 13:17.[4]

We, the *Lovers*, the practitioners, represent the starting point in this exploration of the trifold paradigm, the *Sonic Trilogy of*

1. Satchidananda, *Living Gita.*
2. Teresa of Ávila, *Interior Castle,* 147.
3. Teresa of Avila, *Interior Castle,* 4.
4. Satchidananda, *Living Gita,* 193.

Love, as it is up to us to choose to enter into this crucible of transcendence. And ultimately, it is up to us to persevere through the untraversed caverns of our inner being, uncovering that darkness, those underground streams of weeping as well as those unnamable moments of sweet joy that do come in the light of day (see Ps 30:5). And so, we begin the journey inward, following the faint glimmer of that shining light beckoning us, for, like St. Teresa, we too yearn for unity with our *Beloved*. We too yearn to be "as when a little stream enters the sea."[5]

In this chapter, the journey we as *Lovers* embark upon when choosing to answer the call of our *Beloved*, God, is explored. First, in *Taking Off Our Sandals*, the ultimate cost *and* reward is detailed: losing our self to find our Self. Next, the necessary process of purification is revealed in *Finding God in the Gallows*. Finally, exactly how it is we become one with our *Beloved* through emersion in the *Love*, sacred sound, is introduced in *Getting Tuned*.

Taking Off Our Sandals

A favorite phrase of mine is *to love God most*. Such a simple phrase it is, yet to live it is not. For the cost is our life—the life we may have planned, dreamed, or imagined. What? Give up control? Even approaching such a possibility, for most, is enough to strike fear to our very core. Yet as *Lovers* desiring to answer the call of our *Beloved*, we are required to respond as Moses to God's command in Exod 3:5: "Remove the sandals from your feet, for the place on which you are standing is holy ground." Metaphorically, we too are being asked to remove all that stands between us and God. Notice that we are not asked to go and find the holy or create it in some way. No, graciously, all that is required is to *remove* the barriers, the darkness, between us and God and, in doing so, discover the holy, the *light of all lights*, right where we stand.

Removing those barriers between us and God requires purification, a letting go of the known to allow the Unknown to be

---

5. Kavanaugh, "Spanish Sixteenth Century," 79.

LOVER: PRACTITIONER

revealed. As Vladimir Lossky writes of Moses' journey in "The Mystical Theology of the Eastern Church," "The way of ascent, in the course of which we are gradually delivered from the hold of all that can be known,"[6] is revealed in Moses' ascent of Mount Sinai to meet with God. Moses begins by purifying himself, and it is only then that he "is freed from the things that see and are seen: he passes into the truly mystical darkness of ignorance ... and reaches what is entirely untouched and unseen, belonging not to himself and not to another, but wholly to Him who is above all."[7] Moses walked barefoot onto holy ground. And so can we.

Fifth-century Pseudo-Dionysius described this way of ascent, of coming to God, as an apophatic or negative theology. As we remove our sandals, we too progressively set aside all that can be known in order to "draw near to the Unknown in the darkness of absolute ignorance."[8] As St. Augustine said in sermon 117.5, "If you have understood, it is not God,"[9] so Lossky writes, "Negative theology is thus a way toward mystical union with God whose nature remains incomprehensible to us."[10] And along the way, wondrously, we, as Moses, come to moments of unity which, in their wake, leave us in a state akin to ecstasy:

> If we can neither comprehend the One by discursive reason nor by intellectual intuition, it is because the soul, when it grasps an object by reason, falls away from unity and is not absolutely one. It is therefore necessary to have recourse to the way of ecstasy, to the union in which we are wholly at one with our subject, in which all multiplicity disappears and the distinction between subject and object no longer exists.[11]

And graciously we discover that the cost of our life is not such a grave contemplation after all but as sweet as a kiss from our

6. Lossky, *Mystical Theology*, 27.
7. Lossky, *Mystical Theology*, 28.
8. Lossky, *Mystical Theology*, 25.
9. Augustine, sermon 117.5, quoted in Johnson, 13.
10. Lossky, *Mystical Theology*, 28.
11. Lossky, *Mystical Theology*, 30.

The Call of the Mourning Dove

Beloved, as Rumi described hearing Allah say, "I would love to kiss you [but] the price of kissing is your life." Joyously, he responded, "Now my loving is running toward my life shouting, 'What a bargain! Let's buy it!'"[12] Running, knowing undeniably, as St. Francis of Assisi, that, in dying, we are born into eternal life.[13]

Yet just when we could not have imagined it being more wondrous, along the way, we glimpse the most blessed thing of all: *God has been pursuing us even more.* Sufis describe this blessing in one of the ninety-nine beautiful names of Allah, *Ya Tawwab*.[14] In cultivating this quality, we practice turning away from all that shields us from God's love and, instead, imagine continually turning toward God. In the process, we discover that "the divine beloved is always turning toward us, continually offering a gaze of deep forgiveness and endless compassion."[15] It is why in the 110 Hadith Qudsi (Sacred Hadith), Chapter 1, Abu Ohar records Allah's assurance, "And whoever comes to me walking, I will go to him running."[16]

Similarly, St. John of the Cross wrote of this in *Spiritual Canticle*, st. 31, no. 2, proclaiming that, if the soul is seeking God in love, God is seeking it much more. God he describes as the "principal lover, who, in the omnipotence of His fathomless love, absorbs the soul in Himself more efficaciously and forcibly than a torrent of fire would devour the drop of morning dew."[17]

Are we willing to be devoured? Are we willing to answer the call *to love God most*? Are we willing to take off our sandals and walk barefoot, though our feet become bruised and bloody? Are we willing to release what we think we are in order to become what our *Beloved* ordains? Are we willing to let love have its way with us only to leave us silent, humble, and knowing not? If so, we just may

---

12. Barks and Green, *Illuminated Prayer*, 128.
13. Vardey, *Mother Teresa*, 181–82.
14. Meyer et al., *Physicians of the Heart*, 67.
15. Meyer et al., *Physicians of the Heart*, 67.
16. Dhar, "110 Hadith Qudsi."
17. John of the Cross, *Spiritual Canticle*, quoted in Kavanaugh, 83.

find God right where we might never have thought to look—hanging right there, in plain sight, in the gallows.

Finding God in the Gallows

In his book *Night*, Elie Wiesel tells the story of the hanging of three prisoners at the Nazi death camp of Buna. One of the three was a child. Wiesel was fifteen at the time, and he among others was required to witness this horrific event.

> The head of the camp read the verdict. All eyes were on the child. He was lividly pale, almost calm, biting his lips... Total silence throughout the camp. On the horizon, the sun was setting... Then the march past began. The two adults were no longer alive... But the third rope was still moving; being so light, the child was still alive. For more than half an hour he stayed there, struggling between life and death, dying in slow agony under our eyes... Behind me I heard, "Where is God now?" And I heard a voice within me answer him: "Where is He? Here He is—He is hanging here on this gallows."[18]

A few years ago, a seminarian in the Tree of Life Interfaith Seminary[19] program was a mother who had lost her young child to cancer. For several years, her life revolved around hospital stays caring for her daughter as, slowly, she watched her daughter die. Her seminary experience was her healing journey, as she tried to understand why this had happened and to find God in her gallows. Her journey became a profound teacher for all of us blessed to be with her. She taught us how it was truly possible to *blossom, not in spite of, but because of* as she would go on to help other families with children battling life-threatening disease.

While, graciously, few of us are called to watch a child die, we each have our own inner gallows, inner darkness, where a lifetime of fears, despair, anger, sadness has been tucked away in order for

---

18. Wiesel, *Night*, 61–62.

19. In 2009, I founded the Tree of Life Interfaith Seminary, a two-year program that trains individuals to become interfaith ministers.

us to survive. When we as *Lovers* answer the call, the necessary process of purification begins within our inner gallows, so that the *light of all lights forever beyond darkness* may, finally, shine through. As we seek to approach the burning bush and step onto hallowed ground, we begin to feel the heat of the fire purifying us as all the darkness of our inner gallows becomes revealed in the light of day. Walking barefoot into the unknown, we too may find ourselves asking, "Where is God?" when those unforeseen inner moments appear, leaving us unceremoniously cracked open, raw and trembling.

All emotions arising from the process of purification point us in the direction of where healing, restoration, and transformation are needed most. Yet during those challenging times it is comforting to know, as Julian of Norwich, in The Sixty-Eighth Chapter of *Showings*, reveals, that while we will experience the full range of emotions, we will "not be overcome," and, indeed, if we are able to "love him and delight in him and trust greatly in him, all will be well."[20]

Thomas Keating, in *Open Mind, Open Heart*, describes this process of purification for the Christian contemplative as "perfect prayer."[21]

> When we commit ourselves to the spiritual journey, the first thing the Spirit does is start removing the emotional junk of a lifetime that is inside of us. He wishes to fill us completely and to transform our entire body-mind organism into a flexible instrument of divine love. But as long as we have obstacles in us, some of which we are not even aware of, He cannot fill us to full capacity. In His love and zeal, He begins to clean out the tub. One means by which He does this is by passive purification initiated by the dynamic of centering prayer.[22]

Keating calls this perfect prayer a kind of "divine psychotherapy, organically designed for each of us, to purify our unconscious and

---

20. Julian of Norwich, *Showings*, 315.
21. Keating, *Open Mind, Open Heart*, 92.
22. Keating, *Open Mind, Open Heart*, 99.

LOVER: PRACTITIONER

free us from the obstacles to the free flow of grace in our minds, emotions, and bodies."[23] This process helps to transform the false self, who we think we are based on our long conditioning, into who God knows we are.[24]

Purification is the challenging part of the *Lover's* journey. It will test our grit and the true depth of our desire to become united with our *Beloved*. It will reveal to us the true cost of loving God most. It is also the very part, with the help of the *Love*, sacred sound, that can begin to set us free. For the good news is that the *Love*, sacred sound, is the cause *and* the cure. As an agent of purification, it cleanses away the darkness of the inner gallows, clearing out all that stands in the way, so we may be filled to capacity by divine love and readied to receive any measure of new delights from our *Beloved*. So grateful we become for the divine love and delights from our *Beloved* that, over time, we come to know that all of our suffering in the darkness of our inner gallows was, indeed, a small price to pay for what we have received.

Catherine of Siena, reflecting upon the goal of the human journey as being union with God, described the same when she said, "Clothe, clothe me with yourself, eternal Truth, so that I may run the course of this mortal life in true obedience and in the light of most holy faith. With that light, I sense my soul once again becoming drunk! Thanks be to God! Amen."[25] As that *light of all lights* begins to progressively shine through, we too can become drunk with delight, for now we know it is only through darkness that we experience light, through suffering that we can know joy, through death of the self that we can come to know the Self, the *Beloved*.

So, as we enter into our inner gallows, let's allow love to have its way with us: to use suffering to feel, a little more deeply, compassion for both ourselves and others; use tragedy to grow much like the lotus flower that uses the muck under the water to blossom

---

23. Keating, *Open Mind, Open Heart*, 95.
24. Keating, *Open Mind, Open Heart*, 66.
25. Young, "Holy Women," 411.

because of not *in spite of*, and use so-called death to surrender all we hold dear to find only life in the arms of our *Beloved*.

Getting Tuned

Realizing that the *Love*, sacred sound, is both the cause *and* the cure in the process of purification, we begin to experience the sound current as a kind of tuning fork restoring us to greater harmony and functioning as we emerge from our inner gallows. Our part in this process is to use the *Love*, sacred sound, to train our mind so that our soul, our *Beloved*, that *light of all lights*, may start to shine through us, *as* us, the *Lover*. This occurs as the *Love*, sacred sound, chips away all that stands between us and our full, unique, expression of our *Beloved*, God. As Michelangelo said, "I saw the angel in the marble and carved until I set him free."[26]

In the previous chapter, we discussed the importance of training the mind to rest in equanimity in order to cultivate devotional love. In *An Ordinary Life Transformed: Lessons for Everyone from the Bhagavad Gita*, I describe this process of training the mind using the analogy of a radio. We have many channels on the radio of our mind. There are channels that simply replay the "old hits" of our mental conditioning. There are channels that bring forth unhelpful commentary and others that simply generate static. But there is one channel, or mind state, called *sattva* in Hindu philosophy, where the mind finally comes to rest in equanimity, if only for just moments in time.[27] However, it is important to know we cannot *will* such moments. We can only create the conditions to invite and allow them with our intention. For it is Grace that touches us in those moments and leaves us in perfect peace, stillness, empty of knowing yet full of the Knowing that "surpasses all understanding" (see Phil 4:7).

In such moments, we are tuned by what Swami Satchidananda calls the "universal transmitting station." In his paper "The

---

26. Michelangelo, "Quotes of Michelangelo."
27. Rutt, *Ordinary Life*, 76.

Lover: Practitioner

Function of the Mantra Prayer," also referencing the analogy of the radio, Satchidananda writes, "God vibrates on a particular wave length. You may call it a blessing, or love, or light. He is the universal transmitting station, and we are all small receiving sets. To receive the divine transmission, you should tune your heart radio."[28] Referencing the fourth Beatitude, "Blessed are the pure of heart, for they shall see God," he states that "the real purity is to keep the mind still."[29] And "total purity of mind is the only way to see God. Sound helps us to come to that pure mind. This is the reason why we have prayers in musical chanting, or *mantra*."[30]

But is the radio the signal? No. The radio simply *allows* for the signal just as we as instruments, described in chapter 2, allow for the song of God to be expressed through us. There is something quite freeing about this realization. Slowly, we begin to know that it is *not* our job to create some notion of personal perfection, since, in our True Self, where that *light of all lights* shines bright, we are already perfect even as our "heavenly Father is perfect" (see Matt 5:48). It *is* our job to engage the *Love*, sacred sound, to train the mind so our *Beloved* God may become known to us.

And at the end of the apophatic journey, the mind joins with the soul in complete adoration as all concepts, ideas, descriptions, names of *what we think* is God are released into the *experience* of God. As St. Gregory Nazianzen expressed, referencing Plato: "There is only one name by which the divine nature can be expressed: the wonder which seizes the soul when it thinks of God."[31]

Let's remove our sandals and enter into the darkness of our inner gallows, guided by that *light of all lights*. Let's submit to being tuned by the universal transmitting station, allowing our false self to be transformed so we too may lose our self to find our Self, holding fast to the promise of Ansari of Herat: "Know that when you learn to lose yourself, you will reach the Beloved. There is no other secret to be learnt, and more than this is not known to me."[32]

28. Satchidananda, "Function of the Mantra Prayer," 334.
29. Satchidananda, "Function of the Mantra Prayer," 334.
30. Satchidananda, "Function of the Mantra Prayer," 334–35.
31. Lossky, *Mystical Theology*, 33–34.
32. Huxley, *Perennial Philosophy*, 276.

5

Love: Sacred Sound

He put a new song in my mouth, a song of praise to our God.
—Ps 40:3

"Then God said, 'Let there be light'; and there was light" (Gen 1:3). This first utterance of God in the Hebrew Bible has led many to believe that light was the first element to be created by God. But notice, we must first *hear* the command before we can see. Thus, sound was the first divine emanation from our Creator. Given this fact, does it not follow that, for us to reconnect with our *Beloved* Creator, sacred sound would provide the most direct path? I propose so.

"Sound is the source of all manifestation. The knower of the mystery of sound knows the mystery of the whole universe," declared Sufi master Hazrat Inayat Khan.[1] We, too, as *Lovers* entering into the *Love*, the sacred sounds embedded in the original languages of the ancient canons, begin to know this mystery. More succinctly, we *experience* this blessed mystery in those moments of unity created by the *Love*. Tuned by the celestial physician, our *Be-*

---

1. Gass and Brehony, *Chanting*, 25.

Love: Sacred Sound

loved, our minds become still as our hearts dance unencumbered into a silence where only the whispers of our Creator arise.

In the last chapter, we explored the practitioner's role as the *Lover* within the *Sonic Trilogy of Love*. Here we examine the *Love*, sacred sound, as the essential element unifying us as *Lovers* with our *Beloved*, God. Principally, we address the key question: What makes the sounds embedded in the original languages of the ancient canons sacred? I propose the answer lies in the divine origins of those languages. As we explore those origins, it will become clear why I have denoted sacred sound as the *Love* within the *Sonic Trilogy of Love*. Sacred sound, emanating from the spiritual practices in the ancient canons, serves as a portal into the core organizing principal, that love without end, and thus creates the conditions for mystical unity.

Here we explore the origins of Hebrew in Judaism in *Brick and Mortar;* the origins of Sanskrit in Hinduism in *The Sound of God;* the origins of Aramaic in Christianity in *The Piercing;* and, lastly, the origins of Arabic in Islam in *A Divine Discourse*.

Brick and Mortar

The twenty-two letters of the Hebrew script are known as the *Aleph-Beis* and are described by Rabbi Michael L. Munk as "the brick and mortar and soul of the universe."[2] In fact, in kabbalistic literature, the twenty-two sacred letters are known as "the protoplasm of the universe,"[3] profound, primal, spiritual forces which constitute the "raw material of creation."[4] We could say that the eternal letters of the *Aleph-Beis* are the building blocks of all creation, a creation of which we, gloriously, are a part.

If one reads the Hebrew Bible in Hebrew, this is clearly delineated in Gen 1:1. Here we discover that God did *not* create the heavens and the earth first. Just before the Hebrew word for

---

2. Munk, *Wisdom in the Hebrew Alphabet*, 29.
3. Munk, *Wisdom in the Hebrew Alphabet*, 21.
4. Munk, *Wisdom in the Hebrew Alphabet*, 19.

The Call of the Mourning Dove

"heaven," we notice two letters. The first, the symbol for *Aleph*, is the first letter in the *Aleph-Beis*, symbolizing "God's Oneness and Mastery."[5] The second letter is *Tav*, the last in the *Aleph-Beis*, symbolizing "Truth and Perfection."[6] As Rabbi Dov Ber, the Maggid of Mezritch, disciple of Baal Shem Tov and teacher of Rabbi Shneur Zalman of Liadi, exclaimed:

> It is known in Kabbalistic literature that the letters of the Aleph-Beis were created first of all. Thereafter, by use of the letters, the Holy One, Blessed is He, created all the worlds. This is the hidden meaning of the first phrase in the Torah, 'In the beginning God created את"—that is, God's first act was to create the letters from א to ת.

Immersed in the act of creating the letters, God arranged them in "specific permutations that are the source of each and every created entity."[7]

In addition to the distinct spiritual force represented by each letter, how those letters are then arranged to produce words, scripture, the sacred Torah, becomes immensely important. As Rabbi Munk writes, "Each rearrangement of the same letters results in a new blend of the cosmic spiritual forces represented by the letters."[8] In other words, it is no mistake which letters are combined to create the spiritual meaning of a particular word.

Consider two examples taken from well-known Ps 23. First, the word *yancheini*, "He guides me," from the line, "He guides (or leads) me in the paths of righteousness." In Hebrew, the word *yancheini* is spelled with the following Hebrew letters: *Yud, Nun, Chet, Nun, Yud*.[9] Notice right away that the letters complete a circle with *Yud* and *Nun* beginning and ending the word and *Chet* being the center point. Now, let's look at the spiritual meaning of each letter:

---

5. Munk, *Wisdom in the Hebrew Alphabet*, 43.
6. Munk, *Wisdom in the Hebrew Alphabet*, 214.
7. Katz, *Mysticism and Language*, 48.
8. Munk, *Wisdom in the Hebrew Alphabet*, 19.
9. Scherman and Zlotwitz, *Tehillim*, 57.

Love: Sacred Sound

Yud represents "the hand of God bringing us out of slavery";[10] *Nun* represents "what is holy within a person, faithful even unto the end";[11] and *Chet* represents "the agony of the soul torn apart from itself,"[12] "seeking transcendence and divine grace."[13] As we too allow ourselves to be guided by the hand of God, we contact that place within us that is holy and faithful and, as a result, are brought out of slavery, from a soul torn apart, into divine grace.

Secondly, this next example offers a more linear configuration. Here the word is *dishanta*, meaning "you anointed," from the line, "You anointed my head with oil." In Hebrew, the word is spelled with *Dalet*, *Shin*, *Nun*, and *Tav*. *Dalet* represents the four doors into the inner holy, with the final door representing "binding yourself to God";[14] *Shin* represents "the restoration of all the scattered shards,"[15] our broken pieces being reassembled, our being made whole again; *Nun*, we have seen, represents "what is holy within a person, faithful even unto the end";[16] and *Tav* represents "the sound of God and the sound of man. This is the most precious sound; it is the most beloved. Together, G-d and man have formed *Tav*."[17] So, in being anointed, we enter into the innermost door to bind ourselves to God, where we experience being made whole again and, with enduring faith, unite with God in prayerful sound. We could describe our prayerful time in spiritual mantra practice as an anointing as, indeed, it is.

The Jewish phrase *kol demamah dakah*, literally meaning, "the sound of a slender silence," used by Rabbi Jonathan Sacks in the article, "The Sound of Silence,"[18] might well be used to describe this anointing experience. Echoing our discussions on the

10. Kushner, *Book of Letters*, 45.
11. Kushner, *Book of Letters*, 55.
12. Kushner, *Book of Letters*, 39.
13. Munk, *Wisdom in the Hebrew Alphabet*, 112.
14. Kushner, *Book of Letters*, 31.
15. Kushner, *Book of Letters*, 73.
16. Kushner, *Book of Letters*, 55.
17. Kushner, *Book of Letters*, 74–75.
18. Sacks, "The Sound of Silence (Bamidbar 5776)."

role of silence in chapter 3, Rabbi Sacks aptly points out, "To hear the voice of God you need a listening silence in the soul."[19] Perhaps this is the full meaning of *Shema*, to "hear," opening the most beloved of Jewish sacred scripture: "Hear, O Israel, the Lord is our God, the Lord alone." (Deut 6:4) How blessed to realize that in the depths of "slender silence" we may hear the voice of God and receive a true anointing by our God.

And, just as there is no mistake which letters are combined to create the spiritual meaning of a particular word, there is no mistake which words are then combined to create the sacred prayers. As Rabbi Munk writes, "The combination of letters, as formulated by the spiritual masters who composed the prayers, have the power to arouse spiritual forces beyond our imagination."[20] And just as God created the letters that were then combined into words to create the sacred prayers, so, in like manner, was the whole of the Torah created and divinely bestowed upon Moses for the Jewish people.

As Rabbis Nosson Schman and Meir Zlotowitz, general editors of *The Interlinear Chumash*, write, quoting Rambam, or Maimonides, who formulated the Thirteen Principles of Faith, it is a "unanimously held view that every letter and word of the Torah was given to Moses by God."[21] It is for this reason that the Torah has not been and cannot be changed nor can anything ever be added. Indeed, "the Talmud states emphatically that if one questions the Divine origin of even a single letter it is tantamount to denial of the entire Torah."[22] Indeed, reminiscent of Rabbi Michael L. Munk's description of the letters composing the soul of the universe, Rabbis Scherman and Zlotowitz declare, "The Torah is the blueprint and its study is the soul of Creation."[23]

We now see clearly the origins of the sacred prayers within the Hebrew Bible. We understand now how our intoning the

---

19. Sacks, "The Sound of Silence (Bamidbar 5776)."
20. Munk, *Wisdom in the Hebrew Alphabet*, 22.
21. Scherman and Zlotowitz, *Interlinear Chumash*, xvii.
22. Scherman and Zlotowitz, *Interlinear Chumash*, xvii.
23. Scherman and Zlotowitz, *Interlinear Chumash*, xx.

LOVE: SACRED SOUND

sacred sounds is much more than simply intoning linguistically. We could say that when we intone the sacred sounds, the eternal letters tune us into harmony with our Creator. In a similar fashion to Swami Satchidananda's analogy of God being the universal transmitting station and us the small receiving sets, referenced in the last chapter, Munk writes, also quoting Rambam, "Just as the larger universe was created and survives by virtue of the twenty-two manifestations of spirituality contained in the *Aleph-Beis*, so too, the miniature universe [individual] has his own *Alpha-Beis*, his own flow of spirituality that he brings to bear upon himself and his surroundings."[24] And, being so, we discover what the esteemed Rabbi Moshe Chaim Ephraim wrote in his work *Degel Machneh Ephraim*, "Man has the power to affect the sacred letters with which God created heaven and earth . . . But, when he acts properly, he enables the powers within the *Aleph-Beis* to achieve their purpose and reflect their full holiness. He can elevate not only his personal universe, but that of everyone around him."[25]

And so, as we *Lovers* intone the *Love*, the sacred sounds, of the *Aleph-Beis* emanating from the sacred scriptures of the Hebrew Bible, we unite our miniature universe with the larger universe, our soul with the soul of our Creator, our *Beloved*. And in doing so, we create the conditions to experience what we have known not.

The Sound of God

In Judaism, we began with the letters, the *Aleph-Beis*, and saw how this sonic aspect of the divine is the brick and mortar of the faith. In tracing the sonic aspect within Hinduism, we start with the Vedic scriptures, as it is here that we discover that sound is not just an aspect of the divine but, instead, *is* the Divine. As Guy L. Beck writes in *Sonic Theology: Hinduism and Sacred Sound*, "Sacred sound, in both its speculative and practical aspects, constitutes a

---

24. Munk, *Wisdom in the Hebrew Alphabet*, 24.
25. Munk, *Wisdom in the Hebrew Alphabet*, 25.

centralis arcanum of the Hindu tradition."²⁶ Simply, sound constitutes the basic nature and structure of all creation. Sound is God.

Examining the origins of the Vedic scriptures bears out Beck's claims. Arguably the oldest in our recordings of sacred texts, this vast compilation of scripture was initially conceived and brought forth by the breath of God. As recorded in the Upanisads, the culminating scriptures of the Vedas, the great Vedic truths were "breathed out by God as the breath of God blowing on us."²⁷ This very breath created the "structure of the universe that is reflected in the structure of the Vedas. The universe itself and various things in it were brought into being through the sound current."²⁸ This sound current, carrying the Vedic scriptures on the breath of God, was heard and recorded over many centuries by the seers, or *rishis*, during periods of inspired intuition or enlightenment.²⁹

Perhaps we would imagine that these inspired *rishis* were Brahmins or high priests. Yet C. Kunhan Raja, who wrote *The Survey of Sanskrit Literature*, has argued that the Vedic authors were primarily poets, not priests. Moreover, he described them as "normal citizens in their private life," distinguished from general citizens only by "their special poetic gift."³⁰ The fact that God would reveal the holy scriptures to an otherwise ordinary group of individuals is critical to the Hindu ontological view of God, *tat tvam asi* (That thou art), discussed earlier. It is heartening to know that we too, as *Lovers*, recipients of this *Love*, sacred speech, can enter into the sound current and be, as Hindus proclaim, "carried across the ocean of ignorance by the Vedic vessel of Truth."³¹

This holy sound current, impregnated sacred speech, is called *Vak*. The *rishis* are said to have visualized the mystic form of *Vak*, "which is subtle, eternal or imperishable and incomprehensible by

---

26. Beck, *Sonic Theology*, 5.
27. Radhakrishnan, *Principal Upanisads*, 23.
28. Williams, *Basic Themes*, 11.
29. Chinmoy, *Commentaries on the Vedas*, x.
30. Beck, *Sonic Theology*, 33.
31. Chinmoy, *Commentaries on the Vedas*, 25.

ordinary sense organs."[32] As a result, these poet *rishis*, "who 'heard' the original verses are said to be responsible for revealing the divine nature of human speech."[33] Yet, it is important to note that this divine nature revealed in human speech is not subject to our human logic. Here, we are less focused on meaning and interpretation than on form and recitation. By simply engaging the external physical sound current of the scriptures, organized in phrases or *mantras*, we create a doorway into the spiritual aspect of sound, *shabda*. Writes Cyril G. Williams: "Mantras as manifestations of *shabda* are held to release mysterious power which through inner vibrations open the mind to new vistas of consciousness... The tonal qualities of the sacred syllables can induce phychic vibrations in the depth of a person's being and channel the cumulative power of the sacred associations of a long tradition."[34]

And it matters not whether we "understand." In my experience, when I have inquired about the meaning of mantra practices across faith traditions, a variety of teachers have responded in similar measure saying, "It's okay to know but it's not necessary. Just do the practice and it will inform you." And, to my great joy this has, indeed, been the case. What I did not know at the beginning was that by consistent practice, progressively engaging the *shabda*, I would, occasionally, find myself in what is called the *nada*. Similar to the Jewish *kol demamah dakah*, "the sound of a slender silence," this not-possible-to-describe experience is best associated with complete inner silence and stillness and is identified as Brahman, "the ultimate reality and ground of the universe."[35] Such moments cannot be willed and are impossible to predict. I think of them as a touch of grace that occurs when the inner conditions have been set. Most characteristically, they can be recognized only in hindsight.

Wondrously, it was from this most sacred place, the *nada*, that the Sanskrit language brought forth the Vedas on the breath

32. Beck, *Sonic Theology*, 25.
33. Beck, *Sonic Theology*, 25.
34. Williams, *Basic Themes*, 12.
35. Williams, *Basic Themes*, 12.

of God. As sage Suta Goswami explained, "From the space in the heart of Brahma, the Chief of all Creators, rose *Nada* (unarticulated sound). It is the subtle form of the Vedic *mantras*, and the source, eternal and immutable, of the Vedas."[36] *Now*, we can understand why it is, in those unforeseen moments in the *nada*, that we experience the ground of our being to know fully *tat tvam asi* (That thou art). By setting the conditions with mantra practice, the *Love*, we, as *Lovers*, can return to our *Beloved* through our own unmitigated experience of the divine. We can, indeed, return Home.

And the vessel that is carrying us home across the sea of ignorance is, indeed, the Vedic scriptures composed of varying combinations of forty-six letters, or garlands as they are sometimes called, the Sanskrit language. It has been said that "every letter of the Sanskrit alphabet is an expression of the Divine Being. It is the gift of God to man. Every letter is a particle of Heaven made manifest on earth."[37]

Similar to Hebrew, the Sanskrit letters are associated with esoteric meanings, and, in addition, are said to be "the root vibrations of material creation, maintenance and destruction of the universe."[38] The word "vibrations" is key here, for each letter, exclaims Swami Akandananda, is "based on the subtle vibrations that underlie the elements of the world,"[39] indeed, all creation. As we intone mantras in Sanskrit, we come into harmony with the *shabda*, and the strings of our soul are tuned by God's own celestial fingers.

And, graciously, this tuning occurs on two levels: the practical as well as the esoteric. When individual Sanskrit letters are joined together in short syllables called *bija*, or "seed syllables,"[40] *Lovers* can most easily access the letters' practical applications. For example, two seed syllables often learned by beginners are *Gum*,[41]

36. Beck, *Sonic Theology*, 184–85.
37. Freund, *Varna Siksa*, 24.
38. Beck, *Sonic Theology*, 131.
39. Gass and Brehony, *Chanting*, 69–70.
40. Gass and Brehony, *Chanting*, 70.
41. Ashley-Farrand, *Healing Mantras*, 65.

Love: Sacred Sound

which promotes the overcoming of obstacles, and *Shrim*,[42] which attracts abundance in a variety of forms. Here, we as *Lovers* engage the practical aspects of the sound current, inviting those celestial fingers to bring us back into harmony as the need may arise.

Examining these two seed syllables within their respective basic mantra forms gives us a better understanding of their purpose and influence. I will break out each one and then explain the commonalities.

The seed syllable *Gum: Om Gum Ganapatayei Namaha*

Om—Universal creative sound
Gum—Seed syllable for the removal of obstacles
Gunapati—Anthropomorphized deity, another name for Ganesha
Yei—Shakti activating sound
Namaha—Salutation[43]

The seed syllable *Shrim: Om Shrim Maha Lakshmiyei Swaha*

Om—Universal creative sound
Shrim—Seed syllable for attracting abundance
Maha—Much abundance
Lakshmi—Anthropomorphized deity
Yei—Shakti activating sound
Swaha—Salutation[44]

Notice that both mantras begin with intoning *Om*, or as it is also written, *AUM*. This primal syllable is said to contain the entire Sanskrit alphabet in seed form.[45] Next follows the *bija*, or seed syllable, and then the name of the anthropomorphized being from the Hindu pantheon who embodies and represents the vibration of the respective *bija*. The tonal quality is then strengthened by the accompanying shakti activating sound. Finally, a mantra ends with

---

42. Ashley-Farrand, *Healing Mantras*, 63.
43. Ashley-Farrand, *Healing Mantras*, 15.
44. Ashley-Farrand, *Healing Mantras*, 151.
45. Beck, *Sonic Theology*, 246.

a salutation. Most often a salutation is either *Namaha* or *Swaha*, depending upon a variety of factors.

How wonderful to know that by engaging mantras, the *Love*, we can be tuned by those blessed celestial fingers to attract what is needed in a variety of practical ways and, at the same time, create the conditions to join with the spiritual aspect of sound, *shabda*. And as Grace allows, we may enter, unexpectedly, into the *nada*, blessed unity with our *Beloved*. In doing so, we find resonance with the words of Hans Kayser, a musicologist who spent a lifetime researching cosmic sound and world harmonies: "There are powers above and shapes written in the sky which sound in your own soul, which concern you most vitally, and which belong to the Godhead as much as you do in your innermost self."[46]

The Piercing

"A short prayer pierces the heavens," writes the anonymous fourteenth-century author of the contemplative classic *The Cloud of Unknowing*.[47] There is much in this little phrase that invites us to deeper understanding of how sacred sound has long been engaged by Christian contemplatives.

Just what is this prayer that is capable of piercing the heavens? It is one word, called by Father Thomas Keating a "sacred word"[48] used as a "focal point"[49] to return to when the mind wanders in contemplative or centering prayer practice. While practitioners of Eastern meditation generally engage a scriptural word or phrase audibly, here contemplatives engage the sacred word mentally in silence. However, the purpose and intent for using a sonic focal point is the same. As Keating reflects, "The sacred word enables you to unite with your Source."[50]

---

46. Kayser, quoted in Beck, 219.
47. Johnston, *Cloud of Unknowing*, 85.
48. Keating, *Open Mind, Open Heart*, 32.
49. Keating, *Open Mind, Open Heart*, 32.
50. Keating, *Open Mind, Open Heart*, 32.

Love: Sacred Sound

And how does this happen? We are told repeatedly by the anonymous author of *The Cloud of Unknowing* that we are to "attend more to the wholly otherness of God rather than to your own misery."[51] One word. One sound. Inviting us to allow all that stands between us and God to fall away so that only our love for God remains. For it is in this love, attending only to God, that we are "wonderfully transformed in the interior experience of nothingness and nowhere."[52] When we desire, first and foremost, to love God most, nothing exists, no external reward is tantalizing enough to divert our focus. And, as in the experience of the Jewish *kol demamah dakah* and the Hindu *nada*, in the experience of *nothingness and nowhere* we discover, paradoxically, God is everywhere—that we live in God and God lives in us. The exquisite brevity of this one-word prayer reminds us that, graciously, not even our effort is required, for we discover that love is, indeed, "full of rest."[53] In the sweet piercing, we come to know that our simple loving is quite enough as our humble heart opens to receive the gift of all gifts, the *Beloved* himself.

And how might we describe this heaven that is pierced? Reminiscent of our discussions in chapter 3, Keating writes, "It is important to realize that the place to which we are going is one in which the knower, the knowing and that which is known are all one. This is what divine union is."[54] Keating continues, "As long as you *feel* united with God, it cannot be full union. So long as there is a thought, it is not full union. The moment of union has no thought. You don't know about it until you emerge from it," as we described in the previous section.[55] Yet the experience of this piercing, brought about by our single pointed attention to the sacred word, holding as our only intention to attend toward God, loving him most, leaves us not where we began. All that is left is our silent ecstatic cry.

51. Johnston, *Cloud of Unknowing*, 70.
52. Johnston, *Cloud of Unknowing*, 125.
53. Johnston, *Cloud of Unknowing*, 176.
54. Keating, *Open Mind, Open Heart*, 69.
55. Keating, *Open Mind, Open Heart*, 69.

The Call of the Mourning Dove

In addition to the rich contemplative prayer tradition in which sacred sound is invoked in silence, there is also evidence that Christians have had a long tradition of making a joyful noise in praise of the *Beloved*. And sometimes this praise has been in the form of single words or phrases. The most notable example of a single word is *Abba*, the Aramaic form for Father. As Joseph A. Grassi writes in Christian Mantras: The Rediscovery and Power of an Ancient Approach to Inner Transformation, "*Abba* was a most precious, powerful and repeated word of Jesus himself."[56] In addition, as Jesus had told his disciples in his last discourse, recorded in John 14:13, to pray in his name, Grassi asserts, "the name of Jesus or Christ was also repeated countless times each day for a special need, or a question of special power to accomplish a healing or to accompany a good deed."[57]

As Jesus spoke in Aramaic, it is important to emphasize the relationship of this ancient language to Hebrew. Dr. Rocco A. Errico, Unity minister, authority on the Aramaic and Hebrew interpretations of the Bible, and founder and president of the Noohra Foundation, writes in his book *Setting a Trap for God: The Aramaic Prayer of Jesus*, "Aramaic and Hebrew are sister languages. Many of the root words for the Hebrew tongue are Aramaic roots. The native tongue of Jesus of Nazareth was Aramaic. He spoke, taught and proclaimed his joyful message all over Palestine in his own language."[58] In the *Aramaic English New Testament*, Andrew Gabriel Roth displays the Hebrew and Aramaic scripts, showing that, while the scripts differ visually, the name for each letter, its English equivalent, and its numerical value (particularly important to Hebrew scholars) are identical.[59]

Particular to our purposes, we could apply much of what was written on Hebrew in *Brick and Mortar* to our understanding of the use of the Aramaic language here. For example, with *Abba*, we again notice a circular effect as the word uses the letters *Alef, Bait,*

---

56. Grassi, "Christian Mantras," 537.
57. Grassi, "Christian Mantras," 537.
58. Errico, *Setting a Trap for God*, 6.
59. Roth, *Aramaic English New Testament*, 720–21.

Love: Sacred Sound

Bait, Alef. Alef, the first letter and one of two in the *Aleph-Beis* that have no sound, represents the first, the leader and master of all letters, the prime factor, emanating from silence, in the combinations and constellations of letters that form the very elements of creation.[60] *Beis* represents the blessing in creation, duality and plurality.[61] So, when we intone *Abba*, we are embracing both the "prime factor" in creation and its true blessing in creation itself.

"A short prayer pierces the heavens." How blessed to know that whether we are intoning a single sacred word in contemplative prayer practice, or audibly intoning one word such as *Abba*, we are inviting a delectable piercing by the *Love*, sacred sound, such as St. Teresa of Ávila describes in the Sixth Mansion of the "Interior Castle." "It [the soul] is conscious of having been most delectably wounded, but cannot say how or by whom; but it is certain that this is a precious experience and it would be glad if it were never to be healed of that wound."[62]

As *Lovers*, in those moments of piercing we, too, find ourselves, as St. Teresa describes it, "suspended aloft"[63] and "parched with thirst,"[64] yet we realize we would endure all again, for, compared to what we have received, such trials seem as nothing.[65] Indeed, this is so as, for now, union with our *Beloved* is ever close. Such is the way when we love God most.

A Divine Discourse

Recall in chapter 1, the brief introduction to the story of Muhammad's visitation by the angel in the cave of Mount Hira charging him to "Proclaim!"[66] This unlettered man is referred to by Muslims

---

60. Munk, *Wisdom in the Hebrew Alphabet*, 43.
61. Munk, *Wisdom in the Hebrew Alphabet*, 55.
62. Teresa of Ávila, *Interior Castle*, 93.
63. Teresa of Avila, *Interior Castle*, 143.
64. Teresa of Avila, *Interior Castle*, 143.
65. Teresa of Avila, *Interior Castle*, 145.
66. Smith, *World's Religions*, 226.

as "God's mouth-piece,"[67] the one chosen to receive the sacred texts, bestowed by God, which would define and create the religion of Islam.

Muhammad, who has been described as a "great fiery heart reaching out for God,"[68] would visit the cave for fifteen years in preparation for this prophetic visitation.[69] Subsequently, the words of the holy Qur'an would come to Muhammad in manageable segments over the next twenty-three years, from approximately 610 up to the time of his death in 632 CE, through voices that would gradually be condensed into a single voice that identified itself as Gabriel. The words that Muhammad exclaimed in these episodes of revelation "were recorded on bones, barks, leaves, and scraps of parchment, with God preserving their accuracy throughout."[70] It was in this way that this Divine discourse was preserved in its original form. Indeed, Huston Smith, referencing Charles Le Gai Eaton's *Islam and the Destiny of Man*, writes that on the anniversary of that Night of Power, when the first verses of the Qur'an were revealed to Muhammad, "It is possible to hear the grass grow and the trees speak, and that those who do so become saints or sages, for on the annual return of that Night one can see through the fingers of God."[71]

Notably, this divine discourse was delivered in the first person. Here, Allah is said to describe himself and to make known his laws. Muslims believe the Qur'an is not *about* [italics mine] the Truth but, rather, *is* [italics mine] the Truth.[72] Writes Smith, "The Muslim is therefore inclined to consider each individual sentence of the Holy Book as a separate revelation and to experience the words themselves, even their sounds, as a means of grace."[73]

---

67. Smith, *World's Religions*, 221.
68. Smith, *World's Religions*, 225.
69. Smith, *World's Religions*, 224.
70. Smith, *World's Religions*, 232–33.
71. Smith, *World's Religions*, 225.
72. Smith, *World's Religions*, 235.
73. Smith, *World's Religions*, 235.

Love: Sacred Sound

Since the Qur'an is believed to be the unmitigated word of God, preserved in the original form, it is no wonder that this scripture is called a Divine discourse of such "beauty and splendor that it far exceeds even the best specimens of the sayings of the Seal of the Prophets."[74] And it is said that what is capable of carrying the reader far beyond the literal meanings into the full import of the holy message is the Arabic language. As Philip Hitti, authority on Arab and Middle Eastern history and Islam and sematic languages, puts it, "No people in the world are so moved by the word, spoken or written, as the Arabs. Hardly any language seems capable of exercising over the minds of its users such irresistible influence as Arabic."[75] Houston Smith confirms this sentiment, writing, "The rhythm, melodic cadence, the rhyme produce a powerful hypnotic effect. Thus, the power of the koranic revelation lies not only in the literal meaning of its words but also in the language in which this meaning incorporated, including its sound."[76]

Because the "content and container are here inseparably fused,"[77] translations are thought to be incapable of conveying the mystery the Qur'an holds in the original. It is clear now why, traditionally, Muslims have resisted translating the Qur'an into other languages. Indeed, writes Ali Quli Qara'i, translator of *The Qur'an: With a Phrase-by-Phrase English Translation*, "In order to truly understand and to experience the Qur'an as it was originally revealed, it is essential that it be read in the original Arabic."[78]

Examining the Arabic language points to how such revelation is revealed and grace bestowed, for we discover that there is, literally, no differentiation between us and the language itself. The twenty-eight letters of the Arabic alphabet are said to compose the inner subtle body of each person.[79] In addition, each letter is associated with a particular physical location in the body. M. R. Bawa

74. Qara'i, *Qur'an*, xiv.
75. Smith, *World's Religions*, 233.
76. Smith, *World's Religions*, 234.
77. Smith, *World's Religions*, 234.
78. Qara'i, *Qur'an*, x.
79. Muhaiyaddeen, *Dhikr*, 21.

Muhaiyaddeen in *Dhikr: The Remembrance of God*, graphically displays the location of each of the letters and its corresponding relationship to the physical body.[80]

He writes that Allah himself proclaimed, "I explained all this to Muhammad, drew for him the human form using the twenty-eight letters, explained the greatness within you, your powers, the beauties of that form, and the greatness of man."[81] And, wondrously, this greatness comes from each letter expressing a quality or action of God recorded in the ninety-nine beautiful names of God.[82] And, in turn, the Qur'an is viewed as the "encoded book," containing all the ninety-nine beautiful names.[83]

Now we can better relate to the quote from the Hadith Qudsi opening chapter 3, "I was a hidden treasure and yearned to be known. Therefore, I created the creatures so that I might be known."[84] Each creation, or human being, carries within all the qualities and potentials of Allah. Indeed, we could say that each creature is, as yet, an unrealized manifestation of Allah himself. This is the full import and meaning of the well-loved sacred phrase *La ilaha illallah*, "There is no god but God [Allah],"[85] recorded in Qur'an, Ta Ha, 20:14: "Indeed, I am Allah—there is no god except Me."[86] As M. R. Bawa Muhaiyaddeen writes,

> God's ninety-nine powers, His *wilayat* [the powers of His attributes through which all creation came into existence], exist within you. They exist as the letters that constitute your form. These ninety-nine divine names are what you are. When you have completely understood these ninety-nine names, then Allah alone will remain. When you hand over the ninety-nine powers and give all praise to him, the praise of *al hamdu lillah* [Everything

80. Muhaiyaddeen, *Dhikr*, 90–91.
81. Muhaiyaddeen, *Dhikr*, 89.
82. Muhaiyaddeen, *Dhikr*, 21–22.
83. Meyer et al., *Physicians of the Heart*, 5.
84. Sharify-Funk and Dickson, "Traces of Panentheism," 148.
85. Sharify-Funk and Dickson, "Traces of Panentheism," 148.
86. Qara'i, *Qur'an*, 435.

Love: Sacred Sound

is Yours], then you will be nothing, and only Allah will exist. This will be the one-hundredth name. He will be as Himself, existing as His own power. At that point, only His resonance will be heard. You will not be. One in that state has become Allah.[87]

And so, we grow toward the realization of our true nature, unity with Allah, through the recitation of the ninety-nine beautiful names. These names are called *sifat* and are referred to as "sound formulas."[88] Through the recitation of this Love, the sound formulas, we are carried through two progressive levels of awareness. First, as we begin our recitation, the heart opens to the deeper levels of meaning and understanding referred to as *al-furqaan*, discriminating wisdom.[89] At this level, we receive awareness of how the particular quality is currently being manifested in our daily lives and are pointed toward more enlightened expressions. As we continue with the recitation, over time, we enter into *al-nujmaan*, which means the light of a shower of shooting stars.[90] As Myers writes, "Such a mystical light of direct experience is what each beautiful Name communicates at the deepest level."[91]

Yet in order to progress toward an experience of the mystical light residing at the deepest level of each of the beautiful names, we must go through a process of *fana*, or releasing our identification with that which is transient or fleeting and, instead, identifying with that which is eternal, that mystical light.[92] This requires a dying to our false idea of the self, that we are principally a separate, self-contained ego, and a rebirth into the process known as *baqa*, identifying with our undying, eternal, real self.[93]

And along the way, we open to the experience of the sacred sound *hu*. Similar to the Jewish *kol demamah dakah*, Hindu *nada*,

87. Muhaiyaddeen, *Dhikr*, 24.
88. Meyer et al., *Physicians of the Heart*, 7.
89. Meyer et al., *Physicians of the Heart*, 5.
90. Meyer et al., *Physicians of the Heart*, 5.
91. Meyer et al., *Physicians of the Heart*, 5.
92. Meyer et al., *Physicians of the Heart*, 311.
93. Meyer et al., *Physicians of the Heart*, 311.

and the Christian experience of *nothingness and nowhere*, *hu* is "the still point"[94] transcending all positive and negative elements. Referring to this secret of the secret or the essence of the essence, which all mystics can only point to, it is said, graciously, "God's love is the secret of *hu*."[95] And this, the greatest of all secrets, permeates all creation. As Hazrat Inayat Khan writes, "The sound *Hu* is most sacred. The mystics of all ages called it *Ismi-Azam*, the name of the most High, for it is the origin and end of every sound as well as the background of each word. The word *Hu* is the spirit of all sounds and of all words, and is hidden under them all, as the spirit in the body."[96]

In the experience of *hu*, we are overwhelmed by ecstasy and, in such moments, are no longer aware of a physical or mental existence. In such moments of eternal bliss, we, the *Lover*, experience "the heavenly wine" to which all mystics refer, "which is totally unlike the momentary intoxications of this mortal plane."[97]

Though the practices and methods differ across faith traditions, there is one thing all *Lovers* know, as Rumi beautifully expressed: behind the door opened by the *Love*, the sound current, "There is a voice that doesn't use words. Listen!"[98]

It will break you open and set you free.

---

94. Meyer et al., *Physicians of the Heart*, 3.
95. Meyer et al., *Physicians of the Heart*, 3.
96. Khan, *Mysticism of Sound*, 172.
97. Khan, *Mysticism of Sound*, 172.
98. Barks and Green, *Illuminated Prayer*, 126–27.

6

Beloved: God

Holding me in your loving arms, Beloved,
you have given me the greatest gift of all: Yourself
MARGUERITE PORETE[1]

HAVING EXPLORED OUR JOURNEY as the *Lover* and the origins of the *Love* in sacred sound, we are now ripe to consider the third relational component in the *Sonic Trilogy of Love*, our *Beloved*, God. Recalling our discussion in chapter 2, we detailed an ontological conception of God expressive of a panentheistic worldview. Noting that panentheism describes theologically what the *Sonic Trilogy of Love* offers experientially, we, as *Lovers*, soon begin to recognize the impact of this experience in our daily life. The moments of personal transcendence we experience in the holy darkness begin to find immanence in the light of day.

While God is denoted in the *Sonic Trilogy of Love* as *Beloved*, in moments of oneness with our *Beloved*, enabled by the sound current, the *Love*, we experience mystical unity whereby we can no

---

1. Hooper, *Essential Mystics*.

longer distinguish between us as the *Lover* and our *Beloved*, God. Love, the core organizing principle of the *Trilogy*, has had its way with us, joining *Lover*, *Love*, and *Beloved* in the nucleus of the love without end. This love, constantly circling in on itself, is resonant with Father Rohr's description of the Trinity: "Whatever is going on in God is a flow, a radical relatedness, a perfect communion between the Three—a circle dance of love. And God is not just the dancer. God is the dance itself."[2] Yes, indeed, God is the love itself. Entering into the fullness of the experience, our hearts are set ablaze with a fire that cannot be extinguished. And, irrupting from that holy silence within, our ecstatic cry ignites the Word, the very Word that was with God, the Word that was God (see John 1:1).

In the first section of this chapter, *One and All*, we explore our *Beloved*, God, as the One whom we know in the innermost depths of our hearts and then we explore key stories in *Seeing with New Eyes* highlighting that mystical outcome of engaging the *Sonic Trilogy of Love*, awaking to the face of God everywhere.

One and All

Donald Stone, exploring the new religious consciousness and personal religious experience, wrote, "Dualistic conceptions of God and man are bridged in the religious experience of unity and oneness. God becomes immanent and man transcendent . . . Man is the finite of God and God is the infinite of Man."[3] It is this very joining of the finite and the infinite that creates the conditions for mystical unity within the *Sonic Trilogy of Love*.

Critical to our discussion here is that, as we emerge from our spiritual practice and reenter daily life, we start to *see* outside what was revealed within. Suddenly, we can see this immanent *and* transcendent, finite *and* infinite God everywhere, in stones, flowers, eagles, and in the glance of the passing stranger. Just as there was no distinction between the *Lover*, *Love*, and *Beloved* in

---

2. Rohr and Morrell, *Divine Dance*, 27.
3. Stone, "New Religious Consciousness," 130.

Beloved: God

mystical unity within the *Sonic Trilogy of Love*, now we experience no distinction between us and all creation without. That same organizing principle of love has joined us to all creation in mystical unity, where now, more often, all we see is the face of God everywhere. Graciously, our *Beloved* has given us his greatest treasure, the gift of himself, which we now realize has been with us all along.

But it begins with our own unmitigated experience of God. As Janie, the main character in Zora Neale Hurston's classic novel *Their Eyes Were Watching God*, tells her friend Pheoby, "Yo' papa and yo' mama and nobody else can't tell yuh and show yuh. Two things everybody's got tuh do fuh theyselves. They got tuh go tuh God, and they got tuh find out about livin' fuh theyselves."[4] This quote reminds me that it's all just speculation until we cultivate our own deeply personal relationship with our *Beloved*. Religious leaders can point the way, offer guidance, practices, and support but it is only we, in the end, who can "go tuh God" for ourselves.

This is because there is nothing that can be *said* about God that can fully express what has been revealed in those unforeseen moments of mystical unity. The minute we utter a word, we fall short! St. Augustine expressed this awareness beautifully saying, "You [God] are at once all that is good beyond the power of words to describe" and tenderly revealed how he would "withdraw to my secret cell and sing you hymns of love, groaning with grief that I cannot express as I journey on my pilgrimage."[5] Only in the *kol demamah dakah*, the sound of a slender silence, the *nada*, unarticulated sound, the *nothingness and nowhere* of interior silence, the *hu*, the still point, does God reveal himself to us in mystical unity. And in this revealing God steals us away, wholly, for himself. In hindsight, we may be left with some new awareness, insight, or simply the greatest of all gifts, a full knowing that we are not alone. Indeed, how could we be? For now, we have experienced just a taste of unity with our *Beloved*.

Slowly, this *experience* of our inner *Beloved* becomes more real to us than our outer perceptions of what we may have long

4. Hurston, *Their Eyes*, 183.
5. Augustine, *Confessions*, trans. Pine-Coffin, 293.

thought. As Krishna reveals to Arjuna in the Bhagavad Gita 2:69, "What seems night to others is a state of awakening for the one with a mind thus disciplined. And what appears day to others is as night to the sage who knows the Self."[6] As we go inside to pray to our *Beloved* who is in secret, as Jesus instructed in Matt 6:6, we discover in the holy darkness of our inner crucible that "*light of all lights forever beyond darkness,*"[7] and, in unity with that light, humbly and mercifully, become the light of the world as Jesus told us we were (see Matt 5:14).

And with this realization, we come to resonate deeply with Janie's words, "If you ken see de light at daybreak, you don't keer if you die at dusk. It's so many people never seen de light at all. I wuz fumblin' round and God opened the door."[8] It is the sweetest kind of Grace that opens that door and leaves us, as many poets have described, feeling kissed by our *Beloved*. Precisely because such a kiss comes when we least expect it, we too can often feel like we're "fumblin' round" in the dark of uncertainty in our spiritual practice. Yet what is absolutely certain is that, once kissed, we will yearn desperately to return the kiss again and again as Hafiz proclaimed, "The lover keeps circling in their being their sweetest moments with God needing to kiss His face again."[9]

And from this intimate experience of mystical unity with our *Beloved*, we now can *see* what we were blind to before. Simply, *Lovers* who have experienced the mystery of the love without end in the stillness created by the *Love*, sacred sound, recognize that same love in others regardless of external appearance or faith tradition. We can *see* the love, the infinite expression of God, reflecting back from the finite mirror of each soul. We can say now, along with Kahlil Gibran, "I love you worshiping in your church, kneeling in your temple, and praying in your mosque. You and I and all are children of one religion, for the varied paths of religion are but the fingers of the loving hand of the Supreme Being, extended to

---

6. Satchidananda, *Living Gita*, 30.
7. Satchidananda, *Living Gita*, 193.
8. Hurston, *Their Eyes*, 151.
9. Hafiz, "Sky Hunter," 124.

BELOVED: *GOD*

all, offering completeness of spirit to all, anxious to receive all."[10] Whether we have dipped deeply into the well of one faith tradition or explored across many, we sense more clearly the truth in Philip Clayton's assertion that "the divine in all things cannot be a domesticated God, captured in a single system or set of beliefs."[11]

We know this now, for it is *we* who feel *undomesticated*, unbound, infinite, and free of arbitrary definitions. Father Pedro, the much-esteemed Jesuit leader, knew this. When asked by fellow Catholics why he practiced meditation in the lotus position, he said that he had found God while doing so in ways he did not while kneeling in prayer. Indeed, he described the practices as complementing each other.[12] Finding God had become infinitely more important than adhering to any particular faith tradition's practice.

Yet, as captivating as our intimate moments of mystical unity with our *Beloved* can be, it is our great imperative to light the world with that which has ignited us in the holy darkness. As Mother Teresa said, "Love must be put into action."[13] We resonate deeply now with St. Augustine's reminder that God, indeed, is love and "love has feet . . ."; love has hands . . ."; love has eyes . . ."; and, love has ears . . ."[14] For, more often now, our only desire is to have *our* feet, hands, eyes, and ears be used in service to our *Beloved* Creator.

And so, we wait for the simple, unexpected nudges from our *Beloved* seeking to make his universal law of love manifest in, often, unexpected ways. We keep close the words from the Talmud, "What is hateful to yourself, do not do to your fellow-man" (Babylonian Talmud Shabbat 31a).[15] We seek to follow the guidance in the Mahabharata, "'Treat others as thou wouldst thyself be treated"

---

10. Gibran, *Treasured Writings*, 82–83.
11. Clayton, "Panentheism in the Tapestry," 211.
12. Murphy, "Emergence of Evolutionary Panentheism," 190.
13. *Mother Teresa*, Petrie and Petrie, DVD
14. Augustine, "Inquiring after God," 214.
15. Cohen, *Everyman's Talmud*, 214.

(Shanti parva),[16] or as Jesus said in Luke 6:31, "Do to others as you would have them do to you." Now, when we feel our hearts prone to jealousy, envy, or retreating into isolationist thinking, we remember the words in the Hadith, "A man does not believe until he loves for his neighbor or brother what he loves for himself."[17] Such facets of the Golden Rule are no longer just pleasant sentiments now. They, suddenly, are very real, for we know now that love has feet, hands, eyes, and ears. Ours.

We are beginning to realize the great depth and challenge of Jesus's charge to love our neighbor as our self—all neighbors (see Mark 12:31). Yet it is only in this way that we experience ourselves as the "finite of God" and, simultaneously, experience our *Beloved* as "the infinite of Man." It is only in this way that the "light of all lights" that sets us ablaze may, indeed, light the world. For it is only through this light, emanating from the love without end, that we can *see* beyond all difference straight into the heart of the matter, the heart of the other, the very heart of God.

In chapter 1, we began by discussing the current tension arising between the "spiritual but not religious" and the "traditionally religious" around the question of unity of our common humanity and divinity, and I proposed the *Sonic Trilogy of Love* as unifier, offering a home for both. Now, we know how this happens. Whether from one tradition or from across many, entering into the love, constantly circling in on itself, we begin to *see* what may have eluded us before: God, bowing, kneeling, and praying, right there before us.

Seeing with New Eyes

Because there is nothing we can say about God that would fully suffice, we engage stories to glimpse *tat*, That, to which we can only point. And indeed, every faith tradition points us in the direction of mystical unity with all life: the stones, flowers, eagles,

---

16. Prabhavananda, *Spiritual Heritage of India*, 92.
17. Eaton, *Book of Hadith*, 109.

Beloved: God

and most especially, our neighbors, both next door and across the world. From the stories below, we can see clearly that most blessed treasure to which each is pointing, the *Beloved* himself. Yet we are mindful of St. Augustine's warning, "If we would see God, let us cleanse the eye with which God can be seen."[18] This is our job in the crucible of the *Sonic Trilogy of Love*. Here, we recognize the cleansing required to take to the world with new eyes. It is for this reason stories pointing us toward unity inevitably highlight the human journey.

And as a result of our ongoing healing journey revealing those blessed, unforeseen, moments of mystical unity, we start to feel *his* love as *our* love for our neighbor—indeed, in this way, we do start to, truly, love our neighbor as our self. It may even surprise us when we hear a casual mention of "collateral damage" on the news and, suddenly, our heart aches. Yet as love has its way with us in the holy darkness, so does that same love light our path forward toward a greater sense of unity with all peoples. For, indeed, in moments of true seeing, we could say it is *his* sight we experience as *our* sight.

We begin to recognize how the charge to cleanse our eyes, so we may see the face of God everywhere, shows up in the most ordinary of circumstances to those which challenge us to our core. For God, our *Beloved*, knows that in order to truly learn to love our neighbor as our self, all neighbors in all circumstances, we must be required to find, to see, that neighbor within the full range of human experience. For the love without end knows no exclusions or conditions. Therefore, it can be found, if only in a trace, within all peoples in all circumstances—if we have the eyes to see.

This "no exclusions or conditions" becomes the most challenging in response to deep suffering, hatred, and horrific events. The question then becomes, "If God is love and this *Beloved* is everywhere present, how do we explain all the suffering and, sometimes, stark evil in the world?" This is reminiscent of the critique offered in response to perennial philosophy in chapter 2. The short answer to this question is that hatred, suffering, and horrific acts of

---

18. Augustine, "Inquiring after God," 214.

THE CALL OF THE MOURNING DOVE

evil find their optimum environment for growth *where love is not*. However, when just one person *sees* the ever-so-faint trace of the love in the other, the circumstances, the horrific event, conditions are set for that love without end to transform all in its wake. This is how the *Lover's* personal transcendence leads to a *seeing* of mystical unity with all peoples. We will see this, in both the ordinary and deeply challenging circumstances, revealed in the stories below.

From Judaism, there is a story of how the well revered Rabbi Saadiah Gaon (882–924) learned a great teaching from a modest inn keeper. Fearing all the attention he was receiving was interfering with serving his creator, the Rabbi decided to begin a self-imposed exile dressing simply and visiting places where he was not known. On his travels, he stayed at a small inn unbeknown to the inn keeper. Later, when the inn keeper discovered who his guest had been, he ran to the Rabbi falling at his feet weeping, "Please forgive me, Rabbi Saadiah. I didn't know it was you!" But the Rabbi replied, "My dear friend, you treated me very well. You were very kind and hospitable. Why are you sorry? You have nothing to apologize for." "No, no, Rabbi," the distraught inn keeper replied. "If I had known who you were, I would have served you *completely* differently!" Suddenly, the Rabbi realized the important lesson the inn keeper was teaching him about being in service to God. He knew his exile had been fulfilled and, thanking him, returned home to begin a practice of daily repentance.[19]

This story is particularly instructive as no harmful act has occurred nor an event of extraordinary mysticism. Yet every day the Rabbi would seek repentance. Every day, he would pray to *see*, in the ordinary interactions of his day, more clearly, the *Beloved* right before him. As Rabbi Abraham Joshua Heschel said, "The pious man is ever alert to see behind the appearance of things a trace of the divine. And, thus, his attitude toward life is one of expectant reverence."[20]

I would offer that this can be even more difficult than in times of intense challenge or delight, for it requires us to be ever alert

---

19. Bolton, "The Tzaddik's Repentance."
20. Heschel, *Wisdom of Heschel*, 199.

BELOVED: GOD

when we might normally slip into complacency. While most of us strive to be kind and hospitable, here we, like the Rabbi, are challenged to see the *extra*ordinary in the ordinary right before us. There, right there, is a trace of the divine in the one bagging our groceries, delivering our mail, fixing our car, serving our food, finding the right size shirt. As Rabbi Arthur Green wrote: "Don't look beyond the stars. There's no need to stretch your neck. God is right here, filling all of existence with endless bounty. Look around you. Look within. Open your eyes. Find God's presence in each and every creature and in the unified, transforming vision of all that is."[21]

That "unified, transforming vision" was exactly what Rabbi Saadiah Gaon was praying for each day in order to *see* more clearly the *Beloved* right before him in everyday life. And we too, emerging from moments of mystical unity, find our daily prayer becomes, "Open my eyes, my ears, my heart," as we are awakened to that greatest of all treasures, our *Beloved* God, all around us.

A similar lesson is told in a story from the Hindu tradition. Here we are invited to confront our most ingrained personal images of God, that which we *expect* to see, which actually blocks us from *seeing*. This story tells of a woman who prayed every day to meet God. Then one night, God appeared in a dream and told her he would visit the next day. Happily, she woke to make preparations. Soon a salesman knocked on her door but she quickly whisked him away and later a young girl stopped by to play with her daughter. She too was quickly turned away. Meanwhile, the woman waited anxiously for God in her drawing room. But, by evening, with no sign of God, disheartened, she fell asleep crying. But God again appeared in her dream and said, "My dear, I visited you twice today but you turned me away." She was surprised and said, "It cannot be! I waited for You all day, but there was no sign of You. When did You visit?" she asked. "First I came as a salesman and then as the neighbor's child but, both times, you turned me away without even hearing what I had to say." The woman,

---

21. Green, *Judaism's 10 Best*, 92.

realizing her mistake, said, "I did not recognize You."[22] Sadly, because the woman held a belief about how God *should* appear, she missed what was right in front of her. And many times, so do we.

How much time do we spend in our own drawing rooms waiting for God? What beliefs do we hold about how God should appear to us? To help avoid the misfortune experienced by the woman in the story, it would do us well to remember the words of Antione de Saint-Exupéry: "One sees clearly only with the heart. Anything essential is invisible to the eyes."[23] We see here again the paradoxical shift from what we had once thought was real to now seeing what we might have missed before. The salesman who knocks on our door just may have been sent by God because of a conversation we are to have which will help heal his heart—a conversation that has nothing to do with what he is selling. The child sent may just need a moment of our time, a friendly hug, a soothing voice, a simple, caring acknowledgement that could mean volumes.

It is important to remember that we cannot know how we may be called, for what purpose or for whom. It is why the Hindu mystic Neem Karoli Baba said, "It is better to see God in everything than to try to figure it all out."[24] This also helps to keep the ego in check, for, in truth, in moments of true seeing, we sense clearly that it is not we who are seeing or acting, but our blessed *Beloved* seeing and acting through us. In the freedom of such moments, we experience how infinitely more wondrous and effortless such actions are than any action we could take alone. This is the ultimate gift of true seeing, the gift graciously igniting us in the holy darkness of our inner crucible in moments of mystical unity, the gift from that love without end of which we are now a part. It is the ultimate treasure of our *Beloved* himself leaving us savoring an inner smile born of a joy we could not have previously imagined. It's why in the Taittiriya Upanisad, 3.6.1, we are told, "For truly,

---

22. Pingale, "Seeing God Everywhere."
23. Saint-Exupéry, *Little Prince*, 63–64.
24. Ransom, *It All Abides in Love*, 50.

beings here are born from bliss, when born, they live by bliss and into bliss, when departing, they enter."[25] And so can we.

From the Christian tradition, we look at two modern-day examples from the lives of Mother Teresa, now Saint Teresa, and Dr. Martin Luther King Jr. In these stories, we see how it is possible to find a trace of God in suffering and in acts of evil.

Recall in chapter 1, the story of Mother Teresa answering her "call within a call,"[26] to begin her ministry work in the slums of the poorest of the poor. In the DVD *Mother Teresa*, we see a poignant image of this work as she picks up a dying man from the dirt where he has lain for some time. He is covered with flies and insects and smells so badly no one will go near him. As she lifts him, he asks, "Why do you do this?" And she answers, "Because I love you."[27]

Whom was she loving? She did not know his name or anything about him. Indeed, such details seemed quite immaterial to her. Yet regardless of outer appearances among the thousands she picked up, she knew exactly whom she was loving. She was loving Christ himself. As she said,

> Christian, Hindu, young, old, doesn't matter, when you realize who you are touching, feeding, cleaning . . . as Jesus told us, "for I was hungry and you gave me food, I was thirsty and you gave me something to drink, I was a stranger and you welcomed me, I was naked and you gave me clothing, I was sick and you took care of me. Truly, I tell you, just as you did it to one of the least of these who are members of my family, you did it to me."[28]

Clearly she saw beyond outer appearances to the heart of the matter within all. Pierre Teilhard de Chardin expressed the same. "Christ is the center of the universe. He is the center of humanity. He is the center of every human being."[29] Indeed, he writes, "With

---

25. Radhakrishnan, *Principal Upanisads*, 557.
26. Royal and Woods, *Mother Teresa*, 21.
27. *Mother Teresa*, DVD.
28. *Mother Teresa*, DVD.
29. Teilhard de Chardin, "Christ in All Things," 84.

ever the same brilliance in all, Christ shines as a light at the heart."[30] Surely, it was this light that Mother Teresa instantly recognized in every one of the thousands of individuals she would raise up from the depths of suffering.

She would often say, "We look but we don't see. So, when people ask what they can do, I tell them: 'Come and see.'"[31] And she resisted any presumption that she was different or special. When a Western reporter asked her, "Some people call you a living saint. What do you think about that?" She answered quite matter-of-factly, "You have a duty to be holy where you are. I have a duty to be holy where I am. There is nothing extraordinary about being holy. We were made for that."[32] Indeed, we were. We were made to be the light of the world. We were made to be holy in everlasting mystical unity with our *Beloved*, that love without end.

Some may ask, "How could a God allow such suffering?" Just such a question points to an ontological view of God as being outside of us, a God capable of choosing to swoop down like Superman to save the day. Instead, if it is true that we are all manifestations of the One *Beloved*, perhaps it would be better to ask, "What role might *my* feet, hands, eyes, and ears play in soothing the deep suffering of the world?" Mother Teresa did, and as a result, right in the middle of the world's deepest suffering was joy. As she often told her sisters, "Smile!"[33] And why not? What greater joy could there possibly be than in soothing the pain of our brothers and sisters?

Turning now to the life of Dr. Martin Luther King Jr., there are few more striking examples of true seeing than the charge Dr. King issued in his eulogy to the congregation of the Sixteenth Street Baptist Church after the bombing where three children, among others, were killed: "And so in spite of the darkness of this hour, we must not despair. We must not become bitter; nor must we harbor the desire to retaliate with violence. We must not lose

30. Teilhard de Chardin, "Christ in All Things," 88.
31. *Mother Teresa*, DVD.
32. *Mother Teresa*, DVD.
33. *Mother Teresa*, DVD.

faith in our white brothers."[34] White *brothers*. Can we conceive of the possibility that if someone were to bomb our home or community and kill our children and grandchildren, we could find a way to not become bitter and not retaliate? While we can approach an answer, we cannot truly know until placed in such horrific circumstances. What feels critical to our discussion here is that Dr. King, so very soon after the bombing, challenged his congregation to do so.

I believe he could do this because, as he would say in his last sermon, "Like anybody, I would like to live a long life. Longevity has its place. But, I'm not concerned about that now. I just want to do God's will. And He's allowed me to go up to the mountain. And I've looked over. And I've seen the Promised Land."[35] While his imagery was metaphorical, the experience to which he was pointing certainly was not. Only one who had truly experienced both the intimacy and knowledge of the Promised Land, the kingdom of God, could have risen from the ashes of such despair to encourage others. And as Jesus taught, "the kingdom of God is within you" (Luke 17:21). In addition, King knew viscerally that "unarmed truth and unconditional love will have the final word in reality,"[36] as he would assert in his acceptance speech for the Nobel Peace Prize. He knew because he had *seen* the kingdom of God, the love without end, free of any conditions, within and without.

We can imagine he had visited his own inner crucible to learn how to love his enemies as Jesus had commanded (see Matt 5:44). For he writes in "Loving Your Enemies," a sermon delivered at Dexter Avenue Baptist Church, "So we begin to love our enemies and love those persons that hate us, whether in collective life or individual life, by looking at ourselves."[37] In this process, I suspect he had been called to transform his own inner darkness, metaphorically described as going up to the mountain, to view the light of God on the other side. This was how he could still see, beyond

34. King, *Testimony of Hope*, 222.
35. King, *Testimony of Hope*, 286.
36. King, *Testimony of Hope*, 226.
37. King, *Papers*, 318.

the evil acts of his white *brothers*, a trace of the divine right before him. He could *see* the truth and that truth had set him free, free to love.

Such true seeing in relation to sin and evil is eloquently addressed by Julian of Norwich. Writes Rosemary Radford Ruether, "The central message that Julian understood to have been revealed by Christ's revelations to her was that of absolute assurance that God's persisting love for humans will triumph over all evil, that 'all shall be well.'"[38] For Julian, "all that is, is God; God is the true substance and being of all that is created."[39] And, believing the Trinitarian God to be "all-good in every way," and "because all that is manifests the being of God, all that is is good in its true nature. Evil has no substantial reality."[40]

Key here is Julian's descriptive "true nature." Dr. King did not in any way minimize the horrific act committed by his white *brothers*. Indeed, he saw clearly not just this particular injustice but the pervasive injustice occurring to all his people. He did, however, choose to *see* the "true nature" of his white *brothers* and, in doing so, led the way into the possibility of healing and restoration for all. For, as Julian knew, it is only love, the truest expression of our *Beloved*, that can lead us "back to God as the true ground of our nature and the only real happiness."[41] Such is the gift of mystical unity.

And, finally we look at a story from the Prophet Muhammad as an example of how we might respond, see with new eyes, when wrong is being done to us personally. It shows how Muhammad lived out forbearance, forgiveness, and love with one who publicly scorned him. It calls to mind that "how we treat our critics is the clearest indication of our theology."[42] Here we learn how every day the Prophet Muhammed would walk under a particular balcony in Mecca and each time a woman would throw trash on him.

38. Ruether, *Visionary Women*, 47.
39. Ruether, *Visionary Women*, 48.
40. Ruether, *Visionary Women*, 48.
41. Ruether, *Visionary Women*, 53.
42. Gulley and Mulholland, *If God Is Love*, 160.

BELOVED: GOD

Yet, he never became angry nor would he stop to scold her. One day, when the Prophet realized there was no trash coming from the balcony, he became concerned and inquired about the woman. After being told that she had taken ill, he went to her with water and prayed for her recovery.[43]

Every day. One could say that receiving an assault of trash occasionally is one thing, but to receive it every day is quite another. This is also a clear indication of Muhammad's devotional love, discussed in chapter 3, not just for this woman but for all humankind. There was no emotional reaction. Simply the holding of the trace of Allah he clearly saw in her.

Immersed in such devotional love in response to this onslaught, Muhammad became a living example of the great teaching in Qur'anic passage al-Ma'idah 5:32: "Whosoever kills a soul, it is as though he had killed all mankind. Whosoever saves a life is as though he had saved all mankind."[44] I would offer that it was Allah, that "hidden treasure yearning to be known," responding to the woman through his servant Muhammad and that the Prophet, seeing with new eyes, wanted for her what he would want for all humankind, only mercy and compassion, and so responded in kind.

Jonathan E. Brockopp writes of Muhammad's essence being "tied to a preexistent light,"[45] the first to be created by God, beautifully confirmed in the Qur'anic passage al-Nur (light) 24:35: "Allah is the Light of the heavens and earth."[46] Yet, reminiscent of Dr. George Washington Carver, this Light would communicate with Muhammad through the inanimate as well as the animate. Writes Brockopp, "The inanimate world was made to respond to Muhammad as if it were animate. Thus, a cloud would follow him in his travels to shade him. The rocks would moan for him."[47] Indeed, he

---

43. Patel, *Sacred Ground*, 158.
44. Qara'i, *Qur'an*, 152.
45. Brockopp, *Cambridge Companion to Muhammad*, 28.
46. Qura'i, *Qur'an*, 494.
47. Brockopp, *Cambridge Companion to Muhammad*, 29.

"started to be greeted by rocks and trees—or at least to hear greetings, then to turn only to find trees and rocks."[48]

Whether walking the streets of Mecca being assaulted by a woman throwing trash or walking in the hot open terrain being followed and shaded by a cloud, the Prophet Muhammad, we could say, remained tied to that preexistent light. Indeed, he lived as an expression of that light *seeing* the *Beloved*, that love without end, everywhere he went. It was in this way that he walked in mystical unity with God.

Now, in part 3, "Living the Call: Awakened Mystical Unity," we will examine the *Lover*'s journey in living the call in everyday life and look at key sacred sound practices that engender within *Lovers* everywhere a sense of mystical unity with all peoples.

---

48. Brockopp, *Cambridge Companion to Muhammad*, 32.

PART 3

Living the Call
Awakened Mystical Unity

7

Sounding Our Note

The oak sleeps in the acorn; the bird waits in the egg;
and in the highest vision of the soul a waking angel stirs.

JAMES ALLEN[1]

WE HAVE HEARD THE call and we have answered. Now, the charge becomes to live the call as we awaken to mystical unity with our *Beloved*, whom, graciously, we are now finding everywhere. If we think of creation as God's beautiful symphony of which we have a part, a note to play, we begin to understand the importance of sounding that note in service to the magnificent whole. I think of this note as our unique, divine purpose, for which we have been created. Whether we identify as "traditionally religious" or "spiritual but not religious," we yearn to awaken like the acorn and grow into a mighty oak in celebration of our *Beloved* and this amazing gift called life.

Whether our divine note, purpose, is subtle or overt, singular or multifaceted, private or public, it is first and foremost a *being* state, not a *doing* state. It is about *attending* to our unique purpose

1. Allen, *As a Man Thinketh*.

while *intending* that our note be used in service to the greatest good, known fully only to our *Beloved*. With this intention enlivening our heart, we begin to experience what Gilbert R. Rendle calls an "alternative consciousness,"[2] in which we see meaning and purposefulness that escapes the common gaze and begin to apply "prophetic meaning to common experience."[3]

Allowing love to have its way with our feet, hands, eyes, and ears, we resonate ever more deeply with a perennial Carmelite theme professed by St. Teresa of Ávila: "The value of one's spirituality before God is measured not by the loftiness of one's mystical experiences but by the quality of one's love for neighbor."[4] Why? Recalling from chapter 2 the words of Schleiermacher that every event, even the most ordinary, can be seen as a miracle. Living the alternative consciousness, we know now that loving God most is synonymous with loving our neighbor most and from this vantage point we no longer need wait for the miraculous for now we see it right before us.

In this chapter, we explore the personal journey we as *Lovers* engage in when seeking to live the call, highlighting four attributes critical to sounding our note in loving service to our neighbor: *Joy*, *Clarity*, *Gratitude*, and *Surrender*. Following each attribute, I offer a sacred sound practice known to nurture that particular attribute so we may better reveal, through our daily actions, our eternal *Beloved*, the heavenly treasure silently waiting within our earthen vessels (see 2 Cor 4:7). For as Alan Cohen said, "Awakening is useless unless it awakens the world; wisdom is useless unless it is lived; and, love is fruitless unless it is given."[5]

---

2. Rendle, "Reclaiming Professional Jurisdiction," 419.
3. Rendle, "Reclaiming Professional Jurisdiction," 419.
4. Payne, "Tradition of Prayer," 246–47.
5. Cohen, *Dragon Doesn't Live Here*, 317.

Joy

"What makes your heart sing? Start there. I found the hole in my soul."[6] There is no greater joy than sounding our note, living out our divine purpose, here on earth in service to a greater good of which we are often only partially aware. And each faith tradition points to this fulfillment. Rabbi Arthur Green describes life as a "divine-human partnership" where "human action is required to fulfill creation's purpose."[7] In large degree, this involves *tikkun 'olam*, mending or repairing the world,[8] whereby each lover of God has a unique contribution to make. As Jesus told us in Matt 5:16, "let your light shine before others, so that they may see your good works and give glory to your Father in heaven." In the Bhagavad Gita, Krishna reminds Arjuna that it is in offering his unique contribution that he glorifies God most. "It is better to do your own *dharma* (calling) even imperfectly than someone else's *dharma* perfectly." (3:35)[9] Swami Satchidananda expands on this, saying that each person has been created with a unique purpose. "That's your *svadharma*, your individual duty,"[10] which always implies the benefit of others. And Qur'an passage al-Ma'idah 5:48 instructs, "For each among you We had appointed a code and a path . . . So take the lead in all good works."[11]

Sometimes we may feel, "What can I offer?" To such doubts, Martin Luther offers reassurance, pointing to the antidote of doubt, faith: "It is through faith that one accepts one's divinely appointed standing and lives out that faith in good works of daily life, whether as a cobbler, painter, spouse, or son."[12] Kathleen A. Cahalan called this "radical holiness,"[13] daring, yearning, to give

---

6. Sherblom, "What Makes Your Heart Sing?" lecture.
7. Green, *Judaism's 10 Best*, 33.
8. Green, *Judaism's 10 Best*, 29.
9. Satchidananda, *Living Gita*, 47.
10. Satchidananda, *Living Gita*, 48.
11. Qara'i, *Qur'an*, 156.
12. Cahalan, *Introducing the Practice of Ministry*, 27.
13. Cahalan, *Introducing the Practice of Ministry*, 30.

voice to the fullest expression of the gifts pulsating in our heart. It is a good time to remember that simple, finite acts of faith become infinite expressions of grace in the unseen hand of God.

And along the way we come to experience a different kind of joy in response to the call our *Beloved* has initiated, a call we find is both "loving and kind as well as relentlessly demanding."[14] Similar to the devotional love we discussed in chapter 3, here we encounter *devotional* joy, the joy that sustains us throughout all seasons, as opposed to *emotional* joy, which is fleeting and comes and goes with circumstance. Cultivating devotional joy is what sustains us when the going gets tough and we find our note has gone flat or is ringing out of harmony with others.

Ah, but never fear! What makes our heart sing is actually God singing through us in a language we can fully comprehend if we can listen closely and deeply enough. God has chosen us for a particular mission and has provided for its unique expression so we may ring forth, unencumbered, his love in the world. As we discovered in chapter 4, through the devotion born of such grace, we become less concerned for the weeping that lingers for a night, for we know, indeed, joy will come with the morning. (see Ps 30:5).

From the Jewish tradition, this sacred sound practice is known for invoking immense joy for the most Holy.

> *Kadosh Kadosh Kadosh Adonai Elohim Tz' Va' Ot*
> Holy, Holy, Holy is Adonai our Lord, our God, Lord of Hosts.

> *Kadosh*—Holy
> *Adonai*—our Lord
> *Elohim*—our God
> *Tz' Va' Ot*—Lord of Hosts[15]

This practice is found in the third part of the Amidah, The Standing Prayer, which is the core prayer of every Jewish service. The Amidah is built around three verses. "In Isaiah's vision, 6:3, the angels proclaim God's holiness and declare that God's presence

14. Cahalan, *Introducing the Practice of Ministry*, 27.
15. Rosenstein, *Siddur Eit Ratzon*, 61.

fills the world, themes echoed in Ezekiel's vision 3:12. This declaration of God's spiritual presence, of God's holiness, is followed by Psalm 146:10, a declaration of God's material presence, of God's rulership."[16] *Kadosh Kadosh Kadosh* infuses our note, divine purpose, with joy for the most Holy.

Clarity

Having said *"Yes!"* to the call and to sounding our unique note in harmony with all, we soon realize the importance of keeping the expression of our note clear in relation to others. This requires a delicate balance between honoring others' notes and sounding our own. If we don't maintain this balance, we may be the cause of disharmony. In short, clear personal boundaries are the essential element for creating healthy relationships with others. A good litmus test for *Lovers* to apply to ourselves is the last two words of Jesus's second great commandment in Mark 12:31: "You shall love your neighbor as yourself." Sometimes we forget, or don't feel worthy of, the "as yourself" part. But here we discover the great truth that "taking care of ourselves is more important than taking care of the emotional needs of others, if the latter is even possible."[17] Working to keep our communications, our note, tuned and clear promotes harmony with others and is not only the greatest gift we can give to ourselves but to the *Beloved* we see in others as well.

One of the great spiritual paradoxes is that it is only from the vantage point of our uniqueness that we are able to recognize and embrace what is common between us and others. Those without such clear differentiation mistake enmeshment for unity with the *Beloved* they recognize in others. John D. Zizioulas expresses this beautifully as "each person is otherness in communion and communion in otherness."[18] Simply, self-differentiated people can celebrate the unique notes of others while also celebrating their

---

16. Rosenstein, *Siddur Eit Ratzon*, 61.
17. Drummond, "Self-Differentiation," lecture.
18. Zizioulas, *Being as Communion*, quoted in Cahalan, 45.

own. There is no competition because there is awareness that each note, or unique role, is equally needed for the true fullness of the divine symphony to be brought forth.

In addition, as we cultivate a clear-sounding note, expressing our unique purpose in service to all, a diminishing need to have our voice be the best or the only one in the room occurs. *Lovers* experience such joy in living out their divine callings that such coercion of others becomes less and less necessary or appealing. In fact, *Lovers* discover there is a lot to learn from those sounding different harmonies. This is why it is always best to "challenge the illusion that what we're feeling is the only *right* emotion under the circumstance."[19]

So we begin with the second commandment's "as yourself" part or, as Kerry Patterson said, "Work on me first, us second."[20] For as Hazrat Inayat Khan said, "The further we advance, the more difficult and more important our part in the symphony of life becomes; and the more conscious we become of this responsibility, the more efficient we become in accomplishing our task."[21] Now we seek the delicate balance of loving our neighbor most, *as our self*, for it is only in this way that we may sound our note in glorious harmony with all.

From the Sufi tradition, this *wazifah*, spiritual practice for invoking the divine names as a prayer,[22] is helpful in cultivating clarity of self and unique purpose in relation to others and to the whole.

> *Al-Ahad As-Samad*
> Uniquely One, Refuge for Every Need
>
> *Al-Ahad*—"Uniquely One" (illustrated by the "dot")
> The place in your heart that is so precious to you that you alone can feel it, sense it, embody it.

---

19. Patterson et al., *Crucial Conversations*, 114.
20. Patterson et al., *Crucial Conversations*, 35.
21. Khan, *Complete Sayings*, 215.
22. Meyer et al., *Physicians of the Heart*, 9.

As-Samad—"Refuge for Every Need" (illustrated by the "circle")
The place of the One Being that is the refuge for all, with no limits, a refuge into which it can bring comfort.[23]

When I introduce this practice, I often use an image employed by Sufi teachers with this *wazifah* practice of a dot in the center of a circle. I describe the dot, *Al-Ahad*, as the embodiment of our soul's purpose and the surrounding circle, *As-Samad*, as all the forces of the universe that are there, just waiting, to support our walk when we dare to be our unique selves and sound our divine note. When we become fully aware of this blessed truth, we can appropriately seek knowledge and support from others but no longer look to others to complete us. We already have the *As-Samad*.

Gratitude

The key to receiving all the supports our note, divine path, needs to find a clear, strong expression is gratitude. As Meister Eckhart said, "If the only prayer you said in your entire life was 'Thank You' that would suffice."[24] From the necessary guidance and synchronistic opportunities to the concrete necessities, all graciously appear in response to a grateful heart.

It makes perfect sense to me that if God has created us for a particular purpose, to sound our note in service to his divine symphony, he must have also provided all the outer supplements and supports needed to complete that task. It then becomes our job to "trust, with gratitude and celebration," that God will, indeed, provide "more than enough."[25] This is key! "More" than enough! And, in reciprocal fashion, we find our hearts overflowing as we, in turn, give to others "not out of obligation, but out of gratitude."[26] Our gratitude infuses into all our works a love that freely flows out and back into itself, uniting us as givers with all receivers in a mystical

23. Douglas-Klotz, *Sufi Book of Life*, 184–87.
24. Fox, *Meditations with Meister Eckhart*, 25.
25. Marcuson, *Money and Your Ministry*, 3.
26. Marcuson, *Money and Your Ministry*, 36.

unity of mutual delight. For, now, in such moments that extend far beyond the reaches of our imagination, we are as complete as we are in those sweet secret moments with our *Beloved*.

With trust, we find we don't hesitate to ask. Scripture reinforces this in Jas 4:2: "You do not have, because you do not ask." I always begin my prayers with "Thank you," and often end with asking that my desire be provided in a way that serves the greatest good. I always find it best to concentrate on the *what* and leave the *how* to my *Beloved*. This allows for a manifestation of my desire that, sometimes, is not on, or even near, my radar. It prepares me to be surprised by that which is currently beyond my scope of expectation or understanding. It allows for the mystical. It opens me to Grace. I heard this same principle in the words of a Baptist pastor reflecting on how the promise of God is to provide what we need—although not always in the way we expect. The pastor had found himself surprised over and over again—"particularly by the way God had provided when he let go."[27]

As *Lovers* we remember that we are the shepherd of a vision, a note, a holy task to which we have been assigned but that we are not alone in accomplishing that task. Most assuredly, we work in collaboration with our *Beloved* to ensure that each note to which we give voice, each action we take, each desire we pursue, will, first and foremost, become an expression of his love in the world. Ultimately, it is not about *us*. And with trust we are free to delight in all the ways we are supported in this holy task as our humble hearts can only bow in gratitude.

From the Hindu tradition, this sacred sound practice invites us to open to the victory of Self over self that occurs in those moments of humble gratitude.

Om Sri Rama Jaya Rama Jaya Jaya Rama
Om to Rama, Victory to Rama, Victory, Victory to Rama

Om—universal sound
Sri Rama—Avatar of Vishnu

---

27. Marcuson, *Money and Your Ministry*, 5.

Jaya—victory

This well-loved mantra is called the *Taraka* mantra, which means "that which takes one across" the ocean of rebirth.[28] Yet, recalling Huxley's assertion in chapter 2, what is required for such personal transformation is purity of heart, the essential condition capable of inspiring Eckhart's single prayer, "Thank you." *Rama* cultivates this purity as an antidote to self-indulgence.[29] Mahatma Gandhi, who chanted this mantra daily, learned it from his nurse while still a boy. Even at the moment of his assassination, he was heard to whisper "Hey Ram."[30] In India, it is a traditional aspiration to remember one's chosen spiritual ideal at the end of life. In Vedic writings, this is called the Law of the Last Thought. Perhaps Gandhi was remembering his nurse in gratitude for having so blessed him with this mantra. May we too cultivate such gratitude that only "thank you" is on our lips at the time of death.

Surrender

The greatest, and often the most challenging, of all attributes is surrender. The word itself through a Western lens can carry connotations of defeat, weakness, or giving in, whereas actually the very opposite is true. Surrender is the gateway into the mystical, the possible beyond our immediate understanding. It invites the descent of the Holy. In moments of surrender, we notice a "self-emptying before God"[31] that moves us to stand "naked before God, going beyond what is seen, heard, and thought to a presence that cannot be named."[32] It is from this apophatic perspective that we approach "the incomprehensible and ineffable of the divine holy mystery."[33]

28. Ashley-Farrand, *Healing Mantras*, 148.
29. Renou, *Hinduism*, 235.
30. Ashley-Farrand, *Healing Mantras*, 148.
31. Cahalan, *Introducing the Practice of Ministry*, 115.
32. Cahalan, *Introducing the Practice of Ministry*, 115.
33. Cahalan, *Introducing the Practice of Ministry*, 115.

The attribute of surrender frees us to co-create in pure delight with our Creator as we give voice to our glorious note in his divine symphony. "Free," because now we realize that our *Beloved* is in full command of bringing forth that which has already been ordained by him. We are freed from attachment to outcomes, trusting fully that "what we see and experience each day are glimpses of God's reigning presence, but its complete fullness is something we can only imagine and not fully know in the present."[34] Thank God! How blessed to know that we are simply asked to give voice, form, and presence to our heavenly purpose here on earth, to simply play our part in the creation of the divine symphony and then to leave the rest to God. As Martin Luther beautifully said, "If I knew tomorrow that the world would end, I would still plant an apple tree today."[35] Surrender frees us to do our part, to sound our humble, clear note in harmony with the divine symphony, and to plant an apple tree to bloom for one glorious day in fulfillment of our *Beloved*'s plan.

As we begin to sound our note, we find we have an immediate impact upon those around us as we can also see when it may be advantageous to join our note with others to bring forth melodies we could not alone. As leaders in our community, or simply participants in community organizations, we naturally encourage others to answer the call for their lives and seek collaborative opportunities to bring forth new creations. As facilitators in ministry or personal growth settings, we are delighted to offer guidance in how to sustain the joy born of clarity and gratitude as we cultivate deeper levels of surrender in daily life. We strive to create environments that "give participants the opportunity to explore their own experiences and testify to their own transformations,"[36] as these are the ways that best help others to "welcome the Holy Spirit's activity."[37] Together, in community, we can better see not just the infinite joys of answering the call but also the gifts inherent within

---

34. Cahalan, *Introducing the Practice of Ministry*, 60.
35. Migliore, *Faith Seeking Understanding*, 352.
36. Drummond, *Holy Clarity*, 115.
37. Drummond, *Holy Clarity*, 115.

Sounding Our Note

the deep challenges such answering brings. Together, we discover we can create melodies that enliven, soothe, delight and heal all who can hear.

From the Christian tradition, this beloved practice so infuses the heart with such joy, clarity, and gratitude that surrender becomes our only response.

Abba, I Belong to You[38]

Recalling our discussions in chapter 5 on *Abba*, this familiar, intimate way of expressing "Father" here introduces the beautiful prayer, *Abba, I belong to you*. Brennan Manning, a former Franciscan priest and author of *A Furious Longing for God*, writes in his book of this simple, yet quite powerful, five-word prayer: "Be aware, this is not sloppy sentimentality or indulgent wishful thinking. The greatest gift I've ever received in my life in Jesus is the Abba experience."[39] This practice calls on us to give voice to Whom it is we belong, our *Beloved*. This is no small order. It invokes our hope and faith as well as the subtle reservations detected in repetition. Yet, following the example of Brennan Manning, this great disciple of Christ, we too can find the greatest of all gifts, the courage to, ultimately, surrender completely to the One to whom we already belong.

The oak sleeps in the acorn. Finally, perhaps the most blessed thing about our note, our divine purpose, is not just that we realize it is a part of us or even that we are blessed to be the caretakers of the mission it contains. Perhaps the most blessed thing is the realization that, like the giant oak, it may well continue to sound into the future and impact the world in ways we could not imagine from our present-day vantage point.

But what we do know is if we answer the call to sound our note, give voice to our divine purpose, we will know *joy*. If we seek to love our neighbor most *as* we love ourselves, our life's music will harmonize with others as a result of our *clarity*. If we deeply trust that God will provide not just all we need but *more* in support

---

38. Manning, *Furious Longing for God,* 46.
39. Manning, *Furious Longing for God,* 47.

The Call of the Mourning Dove

of our glorious note, our hearts will bow in *gratitude*. And if we are able to release our soul's song, it will grow into what God has already ordained it to be in direct response to our *surrender*. And all the trees of the field shall clap their hands. (see Isa 55: 12).

8

The Divine Chorus

In my soul there is a temple, a shrine, a mosque,
a church where I kneel in prayer.
Prayer should bring us to an altar
where no walls or names exist.

RABIA[1]

WE HEARD THE CALL of the mourning dove. We answered to become *Lovers* in the *Sonic Trilogy of Love*. We have explored the personal journey of the *Lover*. Now we are ripe to join the divine chorus where *Lovers* from all faith traditions sing songs of beauty to their *Beloved*. Here, all *Lovers* discover, as Rumi said, "The sect of lovers is distinct from all others; Lovers have a religion and a faith all their own."[2]

And, as the core organizing principle in the *Sonic Trilogy of Love* is love, we could say that the principal vow of this sect is, indeed, to *love God most*. For, in doing so, *Lovers* discover their

---

1. Rabia, *Doorkeeper of the Heart*.
2. Huxley, *Perennial Philosophy*, 91.

Beloved circling and uniting *all Lovers* unto himself in that love without end. *Lovers* can now easily relate to Richard Rolle's reflection regarding his great love for Christ: "I have found that to love Christ above all things will involve three things: warmth, song and sweetness."³ Rolle considered these three experiences, particularly sweetness, to be "the height of Christian perfection, a foretaste of the vision of God."⁴ Indeed, *Lovers* entering into the heart of God through the *Love*, sacred sound, find nothing sweeter than the sanctity realized in "the sweetness of perfect love and heavenly contemplation."⁵

In this chapter, we will explore the key sacred sound practices, from the four faith traditions, showing how each reveals its own sweet fragrance, invoking a sense of mystical unity with all peoples. For as all *Lovers* know, much like the soft breath of the mourning dove propels its mournful, sweet, song out into the world, we too yearn to sing those songs of beauty to our *Beloved* in prayer where no walls or names exist.

Judaism

The Shema

"*Sh'ma, yisra'eyl, y-h-v-h [adonay] elohéynu, y-h-v-h [adonay] ehad*
Hear, O Israel, YHVH [the Lord] is our God, YHVH [the Lord] is One." (Deut 6:4)⁶

Sh'ma—Hear
yisra'eyl—O Israel
adonay—the Lord
eloheynu—is our God

---

3. Rolle, "English Mystics," quoted in McGinn, 197.
4. Rolle, "English Mystics," quoted in McGinn, 197.
5. Rolle, "English Mystics," quoted in McGinn, 197.
6. Falk, *Book of Blessings*, 432.

The Divine Chorus

adonay—the Lord
ehad—is One[7]

This most well-known and beloved prayer, the *Shema*, introduced in chapter 5, is the central prayer in the Jewish prayer book, Siddur. The Oneness of God is so fundamental to the prayer, Rabbi Munk writes, "that the declaration of the *Shema* is the first verse a child is taught at his mother's knee and it is the last thing a Jew utters with his final breath before departing from this world."[8] During his life, for as long as he lives, a Jew is to rise in the morning and retire at night reciting the *Shema*.[9]

During its recitation in the synagogue, some Jews cover their eyes with their palm, usually the right, to block out all distractions while reciting the holy words "which express faith in God and God's unity."[10] This practice can be traced to the Talmud (Berakhot 13b), where it is said that Rabbi Judah the Prince covered his eyes while reciting the *Shema*. The behavior was later codified in the Shulhan Arukh (OH 61:4–5).[11]

For many Jews, the practice of covering the eyes is so integral to the reciting of the *Shema*, it is difficult to suppress. One famous story is about Rabbi Yosef Kahaneman, a prominent Lithuanian Rabbi.

> After the Holocaust, he tried to find Jewish children whose parents had hid them in convents and church orphanages during the war. Rabbi Kahaneman would walk through the orphanages in Europe, reciting the beginning of the Shema. Instinctively, some of the children would cover their eyes, and cry out, "Mama, Mama."[12]

This is such a beautiful testimony to the integration of this practice even for the children hidden away from all that would be familiar

---

7. Falk, *Book of Blessings*, 432.
8. Munk, *Wisdom in the Hebrew Alphabet*, 45.
9. Munk, *Wisdom in the Hebrew Alphabet*, 45.
10. MyJewishLearning. "Covering Your Eyes for Shema."
11. MyJewishLearning, "Covering Your Eyes for Shema."
12. MyJewishLearning, "Covering Your Eyes for Shema."

and loved. And it speaks to the power of this fundamental Jewish declaration of faith.

So just what does the "*Adonai Echad*, "the LORD is one" declaration mean to the Jewish *Lover*? Rabbi Green explains it this way:

> You realize that all beings, every creature—and that means the rock and the blade of grass as well as your pet lizard and your annoying neighbor next door—are all one in origin. You come from the same place. You were created in the same great act of love, God's bestowing God's own grace on every creature that would ever come to be. *Therefore*—and this is the key line, the only one that really counts—*treat them that way!*[13]

That *same great act of love* is embedded in the unpronounceable name for the One God: YHWH. Yet, noticing the scripture above, we see it included in the *Shema*. Rabbi Green writes that the most succinct meaning for YHWH would be, "Being, a Being that embraces all of time and space as one, then reaches beyond them into impenetrable mystery."[14] Indeed, he says, "The meaning here is profound. 'God' and existence are not separable from one another. There are not two; there is only one."[15]

It is interesting to note that "existence" in Hebrew is *HaWaYaH*, just a rearrangement of the four letters of God's secret name. Rabbi Green concludes, "To see God when you look at existence is a grand rearranging of the molecules. Seeing the *big* picture instead of the many smaller ones. God is Being when you see the whole picture, the way it all fits together, with the eyes of wonder."[16] Though, blessedly, we can never see the whole picture, for, here, the whole is infinitely more than the totality of its parts. Such is the nature of wonder revealed in the *kol demamah dakah*, the sound of a slender silence, of YHWH.

---

13. Green, *Judaism's 10 Best*, 86.
14. Green, *Judaism's 10 Best*, 87.
15. Green, *Judaism's 10 Best*, 87.
16. Green, *Judaism's 10 Best*, 88.

A description of the outcome of seeing and hearing the oneness of all was given by Rabbi Shlomo Carlebach from the Hasidic tradition: "When I see a flower, I see God's word... The difference between people who love God and those who don't love God is that people who don't love God just see the flower. They don't hear God's voice in it. They see the word, but they don't hear the sound—God's voice. If you really love God, then you see the flower and you hear God's voice behind it."[17] Such was the experience of Dr. George Washington Carver discussed in chapter 2 and such is the way of all *Lovers* who love God most. The love opens all to true seeing where the *Shema* reveals the Word of God.

Hinduism

> *AUM* or *OM*
> "All that is past, the present and the future, all this is only the syllable *aum*."
> Mandukya Upanisad 3.3.1[18]

The great sound of *AUM* is the symbol of *Brahman*, the supreme, ultimate reality. Examining the root of *Brahman, brh*, we find it means "to grow, to burst forth" suggesting a "gushing forth, bubbling over, ceaseless growth."[19] Extending the root to *brhati*, it means by it "eternity, purity."[20] As the symbol of *Brahman, AUM* intones a vibrant self-perpetuating universe of endless purity, a universe of which we are a part.

Gushing forth from the unmanifested eternity into the manifested universe, this symbol of *Brahman, AUM*, commonly written as *OM*, briefly discussed in chapter 5, is said to contain all the sounds of the universe. Indeed, in the Chandogya Upanisad, 2.23.2–3, we are told, "As leaves are held together by a spike, so all

---

17. Satchidananda, "Function of the Mantra Prayer," 348.
18. Radhakrishnan, *Principal Upanisads*, 695.
19. Radhakrishnan, *Principle Upanisads*, 52.
20. Radhakrishnan, *Principal Upanisads*, 52.

speech is held together by OM. Verily, OM is the world-all."[21] As *Lovers* chant the sound of *OM*, one could say we are tuned by the Master Tuner, *Brahman*, our *Beloved*, to realize *tat tvam asi*, That thou art—that we, *thou*, are *tat*, an expression of the One God. As the Hindu mystic Lalla Ded wrote, "My body caught fire like an ember as I brought the syllable OM, the one that says You are That, into me."[22]

And, to be caught afire requires we must follow the example of Arjuna in the Bhagavad Gita and become master archers as is detailed in the *Mundaka Upanisad* 2.2.3–4. As archers, we take up the mystic sound of *OM* as our bow, stretch our soul to the essence of That as the arrow, to hit the mark, *Brahman*.[23] It is in this way that we as *Lovers* hone our single-pointed focus, creating the conditions to fully realize *tat tvam asi*. This is why Krishna repeatedly tells Arjuna, first and foremost, culminating in Bhagavad Gita 18:65, to "always think of me."[24] By seeking first and foremost to *love God most*, we find, indeed, all things given to us (see Matt 6:33).

Swami Satchidananda tells a story illustrating this great discipline in *The Living Gita: The Complete Bhagavad and Commentary*. The great archer Drona places a clay parrot with a red ring around its neck at the top of a tree. Then, stressing the red ring as the target, he calls two students, one at a time, forward. First, Duryodhana, leader of the evil Kaurava brothers, and then Arjuna, leader of the righteous Pandavas brothers.

> "Duryodhana, come over here. Raise your bow. Ready your arrow, aim there. Look at the parrot. What do you see?"
>
> "I see the parrot."
>
> "Where is the parrot?"
>
> "Sitting on a branch."
>
> "Do you see anything else on the branch?"

---

21. Beck, *Sonic Theology*, 42.
22. Gass and Brehony, *Chanting*, 70.
23. Beck, *Sonic Theology*, 43.
24. Satchidananda, *Living Gita*, 295.

"Yes, a few fruits next to it."
"What is the parrot doing?"
"Simply sitting."
"You see all that?"
"Yes."
"You don't have to release the arrow. Take it out."
Duryodhana was puzzled. "Why? I could hit it, sir."
"No, just leave it."
"Arjuna, come and get ready and aim."
"I'm ready."
"Do you see the branch?"
"No, sir."
"Do you see the parrot?"
"No, sir."
"What do you see?"
"I only see the red strip, sir."[25]

As we take up the mystic sound of *OM*, and direct all our attention to our *Beloved*, God, we too hit the mark, the single red ring amidst all other targets. And, soon, in such a state of single-pointed meditation, we taste the waters gushing forth from that eternal purity, *Brahman*, and a thirst is quenched that was, as yet, unknown to us.

And, steadily, *AUM* leads us from the unreal to the Real; from darkness to Light; from death to Immortality (Brhad-aranyaka Upanisad 1.3.28).[26] This occurs as the sounding of *AUM*, ultimately, creates those conditions for us to move from sound to nonsound, the *nada* detailed earlier, or from Sound-*Brahman* to non-Sound *Brahman*. It is in the experience of the non Sound *Brahman* that "men disappear in the supreme."[27] And, having lost our self to find our Self, our soul knows at last true delight, for all questions have been answered: "Whose am I? I am of That. Where

---

25. Satchidananda, *Living Gita*, 302–3.
26. Radhakrishnan, *Principal Upanisads*, 162.
27. Beck, *Sonic Theology*, 45.

have I come from? From That. To Whom am I returning? To That. For Whom am I here on earth? For That."[28]

As discussed in chapter 3, key to understanding the Hindu gift of sacred sound is the clear distinction Hindus make between the mind and the soul. The mind, being finite, is often ruled by thought and emotional conditioning. The soul, being infinite, is an expression of That, *tat*, the essence of devotional love and bliss. This is why Swami Satchidananda describes the sound of *OM* as a trinity: *Sat-Chit-Ananda*. *Sat* is truth, *Chit* the realization of that truth, and *Ananda* is the bliss experienced when the truth is realized.[29]

Let's become master archers, hit the mark, and discover our *Beloved* ever waiting in the *nada* of our inner crucible. In doing so, we'll find ourselves smiling when we read the words of Swami Dayananda Saraswati: "If sorrow is our own nature, then we should have no cause for sorrow at all. We should all be happy being sad."[30]

Christianity

Awoon dwashmaya
"Our Father which art in heaven."

The Gospel of Luke records in 11:1–3, "He was praying in a certain place, and after he had finished, one of his disciples said to him, 'Lord, teach us to pray, as John taught his disciples. He said to them, 'When you pray, say: Father, hallowed be your name.'" This begins Jesus's recitation of the familiar Lord's Prayer. In Matt 6:9, Jesus recites a slight expansion of the phrase: "Our Father in heaven, hallowed be your name." For our purpose here, we will be referencing the opening phrase, focusing on the traditional adaptation, "Our Father which art in heaven."

It is helpful to know that within the context of the Lord's Prayer, this phrase could be one of those short prayers that pierces

---

28. Chinmoy, *Commentaries on the Vedas*, 94.
29. Satchidananda, *Living Gita*, 260–61.
30. Saraswati, *Bhagavadgita Home Study Course*, 165.

The Divine Chorus

the heavens discussed in chapter 5. Indeed, as Joseph A. Grassi writes, "The Lord's Prayer was not meant to be a formula of prayer but a collection of small petitions that could be isolated and repeated often."[31] As evidence, he writes that while the Gospels of Mark and John do not contain the Lord's Prayer as a whole, "They do, however, have various petitions as used by Jesus on various occasions."[32] And, as we have seen in the opening line of the prayer, slight differences exist between the Luke and Matthew versions, indicating a lack of general cohesion regarding recitation.

An examination of the opening phrase, "Our Father which art in heaven," *Awoon dwashmaya*, highlights an awareness of our relationship as *Lovers* to our *Beloved*, God. This is clearly initiated with the opening word, *Awoon*, "Our Father," which is derived from *Abba*.[33] Recall from chapter 5, we explored the Aramaic form of "Father," *Abba*, through the lens of the Aramaic and Hebrew alphabet and discovered it pointed us toward the "prime factor" in creation as well as the true blessing in creation itself. Here, we find that when we add "Our," it becomes *Awoon*, "Our Father."[34]

Choosing *Awoon*, derived from *Abba*, sets a very important tone for the prayer. Errico explains that *Abba* represents a more intimate and childlike expression for God. Quoting Bernard Brandon Scott, associate professor of New Testament studies, St. Maynard School of Theology: "*Abba* is the child's word for father, equivalent to the English, 'daddy.' But precisely because *Abba* conjures up childhood feelings of intimacy and dependency, for those who so address God the immense distance between God and themselves has collapsed. That is, they see Reality as Whole, not divided. Eschatology is realized; for them the kingdom has come."[35]

In choosing *Awoon*, Jesus was letting his disciples know that God was very near to them, in fact, as near and as concerned for them as an earthly father might be. This was in stark contrast to the

---

31. Grassi, "Christian Mantras," 538.
32. Grassi, "Christian Mantras," 538.
33. Errico, *Setting a Trap for God*, 31.
34. Errico, *Setting a Trap for God*, 31.
35. Errico, *Setting a Trap for God*, 28.

prevailing notion of God being an awesome deity largely separate from the daily affairs of human beings. Here, Jesus was describing God as an "intimate, loving and compassionate Presence."[36] As importantly, this Father was approachable. No intermediator was necessary. Indeed, all could enjoy "one-on-one communication with God as 'Father.'"[37]

In addition, when we, as *Lovers*, intone *Awoon*, we are acknowledging our sonship or daughtership with him. Suddenly, we realize we do not have to *work* our way into kinship. We naturally have it because we have already been made in his image and likeness (see Gen 1:27). As Dr. Errico professes, prayer, particularly this prayer, then becomes "the very expression and recognition of our oneness and union with God! At *no time* can there be a split or *separation* from this Presence!"[38] This affirms God being the "prime factor" and "true blessing" in creation we saw in the root *Abba*, transcendent as well as immanent. And we can enjoy the true blessing of this transcendent as well as immanent God here and now, as, wondrously, the kingdom has come.

And this kingdom, here on earth, we can see in the rest of the phrase, "which art in heaven," *dwashmaya*. Errico writes, "*dbwashmaya*, literally means 'who [is] in heaven.'" He goes on to say that *dwashmaya* is derived from the Aramaic word for "heaven," *shmaya*. In addition, the term can mean "sky," "universe," "cosmos," and, by implication, "everywhere."[39] With the full translation of the *Awoon dwashmaya*, we see our *Beloved* God coming into view, as immanent as an earthly father, yet as transcendent as the cosmos.

Hearing *Awoon dwashmaya* had an immediate and profound impact upon the disciples. As John Shelby Spong writes in *The Sins of Scripture*,

> Christianity began when people had a life-changing experience that was associate with the one named Jesus of Nazareth. That experience, which called them beyond

---

36. Errico, *Setting a Trap for God*, 29.
37. Errico, *Setting a Trap for God*, 29.
38. Errico, *Setting a Trap for God*, 33.
39. Errico, *Setting a Trap for God*, 37.

their boundaries into new dimensions of humanity, was accompanied by feelings of wonder, awe and wholeness. Yet, that experience as yet had no shape or form. The best they could do at the beginning to put their experience into words was to utter an ecstatic cry.[40]

I can imagine that Jesus teaching his disciples to pray *Awoon dwashmaya* could have well contributed to their ecstatic cry as they began to experience God directly for themselves. Today, we too, as *Lovers*, intoning *Awoon dwashmaya*, may open a portal into the cosmic *nothingness and nowhere* to emerge silent and still with only an ecstatic cry on our lips.

Islam

la ilaha illallah
"There is no god but God (Allah)."[41]

la ilaha—nothing other than You
illallah—You are Allah[42]

There was a tradesman in a small village in the East who sat on his knees in his little shop, and with his left hand pulled a strand of wool from the bale above his head. He twirled the wool into a thicker strand and then passed it to his right hand as it came before his body. The right hand wound the wool around a larger spindle. This was a continuous motion on the part of the old man, who each time his right hand spindled the wool, inaudibly said, *la illaha illa Allah*. There could be no uneven movement or the wool would break and he would have to tie a knot and begin again . . . He was a simple man and taught his sons his trade.[43]

---

40. Spong, *Sins of Scripture*, 221.
41. Sharify-Funk and Dickson, "Traces of Panentheism," 148.
42. Muhaiyaddeen, *Dhikr*, 79.
43. Friedlander, *Rumi and the Whirling Dervishes*, 25.

This sacred phrase, *la illaha illa Allah*, introduced in chapter 5, is proclaimed by Muslims and Sufis alike. As the story above indicates, the practice of *la illaha illa Allah* invites the Lover into a conscious expression of *hu*, the still point, where nothing exists but Allah. Here, every action is dedicated to him. While its outward expression is simple and effortless, it is born of a rigorous inner discipline. It requires nothing short of the full submission of self to know Allah, the Self.

When the *hu* is added to the phrase it becomes *la illaha ill Allahu*, and the translation is expanded: "There is nothing other than You, O God! Only You are Allah."[44] This particular recitation is called the *kalimah*, or affirmation of faith, described as Allah's grace and pure light of truth which cleanses the inner heart.[45] Here, with the recitation of this sacred phrase, we are invited ever deeper into the mystery of *hu*, as Muhammad Raheeem Bawa Muhaiyaddeen writes, "The One who is in secret must be understood through the secret *Allahu*. That is the wisdom of the secret path, a place which the mind and desire cannot reach. Know Him as you go within. Realize that secret. Only He is *Allahu*."[46] Addressing the full meaning of the phrase, he writes, "*La illaha* is the manifestation of creation. *Ill Allahu* is the essence."[47] To which Rumi eloquently responded, "The lover is visible and the Beloved invisible—Who ever saw such a love in all the world?"[48]

Now we approach the full meaning of *tawhid*, "the unity of God,"[49] discussed in chapter 3, as *tawhid* is based on this affirmation of faith inherent in *la illaha illa Allah(u)*. Indeed, as the manifestation of creation, Allah is nearer to us than our jugular vein (Qur'an, Qaf 50:16),[50] and, as the essence, is the "Lord of all

---

44. Muhaiyaddeen, *Dhikr*, 124.
45. Muhaiyaddeen, *Dhikr*, 122.
46. Muhaiyaddeen, *Dhikr*, 27.
47. Muhaiyaddeen, *Dhikr*, 124.
48. Friedlander, *Rumi and the Whirling Dervishes*, 66.
49. Sharify-Funk and Dickson, "Traces of Panentheism," 148.
50. Qara'i, *Qur'an*, 733.

THE DIVINE CHORUS

the worlds" (Qur'an, al-Fatihah 1:2).[51] Sufi mystic Ibn al-Arabi asserted that these two states are complementary, that the Qur'an "is communicating the truth of the matter: God is simultaneously transcendent and immanent."[52]

So, just like the tradesman, *Lovers* engage in *dhikr*,[53] the remembrance of God, by silently repeating *la illaha illa Allah* while going about their daily tasks. In this way, they cleanse the heart to make it ready for *hu*. As thirteenth-century Mahmud Shabistari said, "Sweep out the chamber of your heart. Make it ready to be the dwelling place of the Beloved. When you depart out, He will enter it. In you, void of yourself, will He display His beauties."[54]

And the *Lover*, who ardently carries *dhikr* in his heart, finds such beauties appearing unexpectedly in the most unforeseen of places. One of the most beautiful examples of Allah entering into the heart in response to the *Love*, sacred sound, is the story of Rumi's awakening, which would portend the beginning of the Mevlevi Order of Sufis known as the Whirling Dervishes.

> One day as he [Rumi] walked by the goldbeater's shop, he heard the hammers of the apprentices pounding the rough sheets of gold into beautiful objects. With each step, he repeated the name of God; and now with the sound of the hammers beating gold, all he heard was 'Allah, Allah.'
>
> 'Allah, Allah,' became every sound he heard, and he began to whirl in ecstasy in the middle of the street. He unfolded his arms like a fledgling bird, clasped his robe, tilted his head back, and whirled, whirled, whirled to the sound of "Allah" that came forth from his heart and the very wind he created by his movement.[55]

Becoming lost in the moment, within the sound, we could say, was the full embodiment of *la illaha illa Allah*, much like with the

---

51. Qara'i, *Qur'an*, 1.
52. Sharify-Funk and Dickson, "Traces of Panentheism," 151.
53. Muhaiyaddeen, *Dhikr*, 116.
54. Friedlander, *Rumi and the Whirling Dervishes*, 34.
55. Friedlander, *Rumi and the Whirling Dervishes*, 62.

tradesman spinning wool. And it invokes the *Adhan*, the call to prayer: "God is great. I bear witness that there is no god but God. I bear witness that Muhammad is His Prophet. Come to prayer. Come to success. God is great. There is no god but God."[56] *La illaha illa Allah.*

As *Lovers* let's pray, as with Rumi, that the *Love*, sacred sound, will have its way with us, for as he reminded us, "Lose yourself, Lose yourself in this love. When you lose yourself in this love, you will find everything."[57] And, how could we not? We have witnessed the *Lover's* journey from self to Self, from darkness to light, from perceived separation to realized unity. We have journeyed to hear God's voice in the flower, to see only the red ring, to know the kingdom has come, and, at last, to release our fledgling hearts to whirl unconstrained in ecstasy. And our hearts are glad.

---

56. Friedlander, *Rumi and the Whirling Dervishes*, 79.
57. Rumi, *In the Arms*, 150.

Conclusion

LOVERS ACROSS FAITH TRADITIONS share a fierce yearning for God. While beliefs and practices differ, what ignites the human heart to quest for the unknowable, the holy, the mystery just beyond understanding, is the same. Today this quest is being most loudly articulated by those identifying as "spiritual but not religious." Yet those "traditionally religious" have long journeyed, labored, and aspired to know God within the lineages of ancient, sacred traditions. While, on the surface, it would appear that *Lovers* from these two groups are moving in different directions, their quest is the same. Within the *Sonic Trilogy of Love*, all *Lovers* encounter the epic human journey inherent in the quest for God, as well as moments of mystical unity inherent in the universality of the *experience* of God.

In order for there to be such universality in the experience of God, there must be, ontologically, universal elements within the One, to which all traditions point, eliciting this common response. Perennial philosophy describes such universal elements, three of which we have highlighted: the assertion of one divine reality; the notion that all of life can be seen as miraculous as soon as the religious view, born of love, becomes dominant; and, the belief that observable practical consequences naturally emanate from religious experience when an individual is in touch with that germinal higher part of himself. The more recent worldview of panentheism has emerged to provide a new context for holding this universality of experience encompassing both the immanent and the transcendent qualities of God. Simply, there is nowhere God is not *if* the *Lover* has the eyes to see.

Examining the origins of the historical canons reveals this universality brought forth by the *Love*, the sound current, embedded within the languages themselves: Hebrew, Sanskrit, Aramaic, and Arabic. The four traditions we have engaged all claim possession of the Word as was originally revealed, yet, as we have seen, each tradition expresses, through the key sacred sound practices, common themes pointing to the One: the *Shema, AUM, Awoon dwashmaya*, and *La illaha illa Allah*. Hence, rabbis, swamis, priests or ministers, imams or shaykhs, and *Lovers* across traditions emerge from the *kol demamah dakah, nada, nothingness and nowhere*, and *hu*, humbled with awe and able to speak in the language only *Lovers* know, silence. Yet now, having experienced just a glimpse of the mystery, each starts to see the face of God everywhere, immanent in stones, flowers, eagles, and in the eyes of neighbors, as well as transcendent in the secrets of those very stones, the silent unfolding of the flower's petals, the wind lifting the eagle from its nest, and, most of all, in the love igniting our hearts when we pause long enough to *see* the face of our neighbor.

As *Lovers* everywhere hear the call of the mourning dove, each is invited to answer and fulfill a unique part in the *Beloved*'s plan for creation. In doing so, *Lovers* discover the joy of harmonizing their notes in service to the divine symphony. Wondrously, they realize that unity with all does not dissolve particularity; rather, it requires and celebrates it. As *Lovers* enter into the *Love*, the sacred sound practices, within the *Sonic Trilogy of Love*, they experience a cleansing of all that stands in the way of this unique expression of particularity and, slowly, emerge to sound their own note in service to a greater good known only to the *Beloved*. It is in this way that *Lovers*, whether diving deep into the sound currents of a single tradition or engaging sacred sound practices across faith traditions, discover their unique place in God's creation intimately woven into the web of life. Simply, each is one *and* all.

As love, that core organizing principle uniting *Lover, Love,* and *Beloved* in mystical unity, has its way with us, we hear the call

Conclusion

piercing the open sky and we respond as only *Lovers* can, propelled by a yearning we can't ignore. Nothing short of feeling the palpable embrace of our *Beloved* will suffice now. Nothing short of finding our own ecstatic cry escaping unrestrained and free will satisfy. The *Love* has stirred our awakening and we can hear now the sound of God chiming softly in the wind as we are gently rocked by a kind of lullaby known only to our *Beloved*.

And, as dusk silently descends, we hear the mourning doves sing.

Bibliography

Allen, James. *As a Man Thinketh*. Oxford: Benediction Classics, 2018.
Artson, Bradley Shavit. "Holy, Holy, Holy! Jewish Affirmations of Panentheism." In *Panentheism across the World's Traditions*, edited by Loriliai Biernacki and Philip Clayton, 18–36. New York: Oxford University Press, 2014.
Ashley-Farrand, Thomas. *Healing Mantras: Using Sound Affirmations for Personal Power, Creativity, and Healing*. New York: Ballantine, 1999.
Augustine. *Confessions*. Translated by Henry Chadwick. New York: Oxford University Press, 2008.
Augustine. *Confessions*. Translated by R. S. Pine-Coffin. New York: Penguin, 1961.
Augustine. "Inquiring after God when Meditating on Scripture." In *Inquiring after God: Classic and Contemporary Readings*, edited by Ellen T. Charry, 207–32. Malden, MA: Blackwell, 2000.
Augustine. *The Trinitarian Controversy*. Translated by William G. Rusch. Minneapolis: Fortress, 1980.
Baker-Fletcher, Karen. *Dancing with God: The Trinity from a Womanist Perspective*. Atlanta: Chalice, 2006.
Barks, Coleman and Michael Green, eds. *The Illuminated Prayer: The Five Times Prayer of the Sufis*. New York: Random House, 2000.
Beck, Guy L. *Sonic Theology: Hinduism and Sacred Sound*. Columbia: University of South Carolina Press, 1993.
Biernacki, Loriliai. "Introduction: Panentheism Outside the Box." In *Panentheism across the World's Traditions*, edited by Loriliai Biernacki and Philip Clayton, 1–17. New York: Oxford University Press, 2014.
Bolton, Tuvia. "A Tzaddik's Repentance." https://www.chabad.org/library/article_cdo/aid/45302/jewish/A-Tzaddiks-Repentance.htm.
Brockopp, Jonathan E. *The Cambridge Companion to Muhammad*. Cambridge Companions to Religion. New York: Cambridge University Press, 2010.
Cahalan, Kathleen, A. *Introducing the Practice of Ministry*. Collegeville, MN: Liturgical, 2010.
Chapman, Arundel J. *An Introduction to Schleiermacher*. Bedford, UK: Harpur Printing Works, 1932.

Bibliography

Chinmoy, Sri. *Commentaries on the Vedas, the Upanishads and the Bhagavad Gita*. Jamaica, NY: Aum,1996.

Chittick, William C. *The Sufi Path of Knowledge*. Albany: State University of New York Press, 1989.

Clark, Glenn. *The Man Who Talks with the Flowers: The Life Story of Dr. George Washington Carver*. Austin, MN: Macalester Park, 2007.

Clayton, Philip. "Panentheism in the Tapestry of Traditions." In *Panentheism across the World's Traditions*, edited by Loriliai Biernacki and Philip Clayton, 200–12. New York: Oxford University Press, 2014.

Cohen, Abraham, ed. *Everyman's Talmud: The Major Teachings of the Rabbinic Sages*. New York: Random House, 1975.

Cohen, Alan. *The Dragon Doesn't Live Here Anymore*. New York: Ballantine, 1990.

Coogan, Michael D., ed. *The New Oxford Annotated Bible*. New York: Oxford University Press, 2001.

Cousins, Ewert H. "Trinity and World Religions." *JES* 7, no.3 (Summer 1970) 476–98.

Dhar, Abu, translator. "110 Hadith Qudsi." *The Hadith Library*. http://ahadith.co.uk/chapter.php?cid=144

Douglas-Klotz, Neil. *The Sufi Book of Life: 99 Pathways of the Heart for the Modern Dervish*. New York: Penguin, 2005.

Drummond, Sarah B. *Holy Clarity: The Practice of Planning and Evaluation*. Herndon, VA: Alban Institute, 2009.

———. "Self-Differentiation." Lecture, Andover Newton Theological School, Newton Centre, MA, March 2, 2016.

Eaton, Charles Le Gai, ed. *The Book of Hadith*. Translated by Mahmoud Mostafa. Watsonville, CA: Book Foundation, 2008.

Errico, Rocco A. *Setting a Trap for God: The Aramaic Prayer of Jesus*. Unity Village, MO: Unity House, 1997.

Falk, Marcia. *The Book of Blessings: New Jewish Prayers for Daily Life, the Sabbath and the New Moon Festival*. New York: HarperCollins, 1996.

Fox, Matthew. *Meditations with Meister Eckhart*. Rochester, VT: Bear & Company, 1983.

Freund, Peter F., trans. *Varna Siksa: The Qualities, Colors, Genders and Devatas of the Letters of the Sanskrit Alphabet*. Fairfield, IA: Golden Meteor, 2015.

Friedlander, Shems. *Rumi and the Whirling Dervishes*. New York: Parabola, 2003.

Gass, Robert, and Kathleen Brehony. *Chanting: Discovering Spirit in Sound*. New York: Broadway, 1999.

Gibran, Kahlil. *The Treasured Writings of Kahlil Gibran*. Edited by Andrew Dib Sherfan. Edison, NJ: Castle, 1975.

Grassi, Joseph A. "Christian Mantras: The Rediscovery and Power of an Ancient Approach to Inner Christian Transformation." *Worship* 49, no.9 (November 1975) 530–42.

Bibliography

Green, Arthur. *Judaism's 10 Best Ideas: A Brief Guide for Seekers*. Woodstock, VT: Jewish Lights, 2015.

Gulley, Philip, and James Mulholland. *If God Is Love: Rediscovering Grace in an Ungracious World*. New York: HarperCollins, 2005.

Hafiz. "The Sky Hunter." In *The Gift: Poems by Hafiz the Great Sufi Master*. Translated by Daniel Ladinsky. New York: Penguin Books, 1999.

Heim, S. Mark. "Otherness and Wonder: A Christian Experiences Moksha." In "My Neighbor's Faith: Stories of Interreligious Encounter, Growth, and Transformation," edited by Jennifer Howe Peace, Or N. Rose and Gregory Mobley, 192–96. Maryknoll, New York: Orbis, 2012.

———. "The Pluralism of Religious Ends Dreams Fulfilled." *Religion Online*. (January 2015) http://www.religion-online.org/article/the-pluralism-of-religious-ends-dreams-fulfilled/

Heschel, Abraham Joshua, *The Wisdom of Heschel*. Edited by Ruth M. Goodhill. New York: Farrar, Straus and Giroux, 1975.

Heyward, Carter Isabel. *The Redemption of God: A Theology of Mutual Relation*. Eugene, OR: Wipf and Stock, 2010.

Hood, Ralph W. Jr. "The Mystical Self: Lost and Found." *International Journal for the Psychology of Religion* 12, no.1 (2002) 1–14.

Hooper, Richard, ed. *The Essential Mystics, Poets, Saints and Sages: A Wisdom Treasury*. Charlottesville, VA: Hampton Roads, 2013.

———. *Hymns to the Beloved: The Poetry, Prayers and Wisdom of the World's Great Mystics*. Sedona, AZ: Sanctuary, 2010.

Hope, Ronald. "Aldous Huxley's Philosophy." *Contemporary Review* 278, no.1621 (February 2001) 102–106. *Religion and Philosophy Collection*, EBSCO*host*.

Hurston, Zora Neale. *Their Eyes Were Watching God*. New York: Harper & Row, 1965.

Huxley, Aldous. *The Perennial Philosophy*. New York: Harper & Brothers, 1945.

James, William. *The Works of William James: The Varieties of Religious Experience*. Edited by Burkhardt, Frederick H., Fredson Bowers, and Ignas K. Skrupskelis. Cambridge, MA: Harvard University Press, 1985.

Johnson, E. A. *Quest for the Living God: Mapping Frontiers in the Theology of God*. New York: Continuum, 2007.

Johnston, William, ed. *The Cloud of Unknowing & the Book of Privy Counseling*. New York: Random House, 2005.

Julian of Norwich. *Julian of Norwich: Showings*. Translated by Edmund Colledge and James Walsh. Mahwah, NJ: Paulist, 1978.

Kabir. *The Bijak of Kabir*. Translated by Linda Hess and Shukdeo Singh. New York: Oxford University Press, 2002.

Katz, Steven T., ed. *Mysticism and Language*. New York: Oxford University Press, 1992.

Kavanaugh, Kieran. "Spanish Sixteenth Century: Carmel and Surrounding Movements." In *Christian Spirituality: Post-Reformation and Modern*, edited by Louis Dupre and Don E. Saliers, 69–90. New York: Crossroad, 1991.

Bibliography

Keating, Thomas. *Open Mind, Open Heart.* New York: Continuum International, 2008.

Keller, Catherine. "The Body of Panentheism." In *Panentheism Across the World's Traditions,* edited by Loriliai Biernacki and Philip Clayton, 63–82. New York: Oxford University Press, 2014.

Khan, Hazrat Inayat. *The Complete Sayings of Hazrat Inayat Khan.* New Lebanon, NY: Omega, 1978.

———. *The Mysticism of Sound and Music: The Sufi Teachings of Hazrat Inayat Khan.* Boston. Shambhala, 1996.

King, Martin Luther, Jr. *The Papers of Martin Luther King, Jr.* Vol. 4. Edited by Clayborne Carson. Berkeley: University of California Press, 2000.

———. *A Testimony of Hope: The Essential Writings of Martin Luther King, Jr.* Edited by James Melvin Washington. New York: HarperCollins, 1986.

Knowles, Elizabeth, ed. *Oxford Dictionary of Quotations.* New York: Oxford University Press, 2009.

Kushner, Lawrence. *The Book of Letters: A Mystical Alef-bait.* Woodstock, VT: Jewish Lights, 1990.

Kwiecien, Ilona. "Report on The Parliament of World Religions 2015 Conference." Lecture, Tree of Life Interfaith Temple, Amherst, NH, December 6, 2015.

Linge, David E. "Mysticism, Poverty and Reason in the Thought of Meister Eckhart." *JAAR* 46, no.4 (December 1978) 465–88.

Lossky, Vladimir. *Mystical Theology of the Eastern Church.* Cambridge, UK: James Clark & Co., 2005.

Manning, Brennan. *The Furious Longing for God.* Colorado Springs: David C. Cook, 2009.

Marcuson, Margaret J. *Money and Your Ministry: Balance the Books While Keeping Your Balance.* Portland, OR: Marcuson Leadership Circle, 2014.

McGinn, Bernard. "The English Mystics." In *Christian Spirituality: High Middle Ages and Reformation,* edited by Jill Raitt, 194–207. New York: Crossroad, 1987.

———. *The Mystical Thought of Meister Eckhart: The Man from Whom God Hid Nothing.* New York: Crossroad, 2001.

Meyer, Wali Ali, Bilal Hyde, Faisal Muqaddam, and Shabda Kahn. *Physicians of the Heart:A Sufi View of the Ninety-Nine Names of Allah.* San Francisco: Sufi Ruhaniat International, 2011.

Michelangelo, "Michelangelo: Paintings, Sculptures, Biograpy." https://www.michelangelo.org/michelangelo-quotes.jsp.

Migliore, Daniel, L. *Faith Seeking Understanding: An Introduction to Christian Theology.* Grand Rapids, MI: William B. Eerdmans, 2004.

Moody, Linda A. *Women Encounter God: Theologies Across Boundaries of Difference.* Eugene, OR: Wipf and Stock, 2003.

Mother Teresa. Directed by Jeanette Petrie and Ann Petrie. Petrie Productions, 1986. DVD. New York, 1986.

Bibliography

Muhaiyaddeen, M. R. Bawa. *Dhikr: The Remembrance of God*. Philadelphia: Fellowship, 1999.

Munk, Michael L. *The Wisdom in the Hebrew Alphabet: The Sacred Letters as a Guide to Jewish Deed and Thought*. Brooklyn, NY: Mesorah, 2012.

Murphy, Michael. "The Emergence of Evolutionary Panentheism." In *Panentheism across the World's Traditions*, edited by Loriliai Biernacki and Philip Clayton, 177–99. New York: Oxford University Press, 2014.

MyJewishLearning. "Covering Your Eyes for Shema." http://www.myjewishlearning.com/article/ask-the-expert-covering-your-eyes-for-shema/

Olson, Roger E. "A Postconservative Evangelical Response to Panentheism." *Evangelical Quarterly* 85, no. 4 (October 2013) 328–337.

Patel, Eboo. *Sacred Ground: Pluralism, Prejudice and the Promise of America*. Boston: Beacon, 2012.

Patterson, Kerry, Joseph Grenny, Ron McMillian, and Al Switzer. *Crucial Conversations: Tools for Talking When the Stakes Are High*. New York: McGraw Hill, 2012.

Payne, Steven. "The Tradition of Prayer in Teresa and John of the Cross." In *Spiritual Traditions for the Contemporary Church*, edited by Robin Maas and Gabriel O'Donnell, 235–58. Nashville, TN: Abingdon, 1990.

Pingale, Charudatta, translator. "Seeing God Everywhere." Hinduism for Kids. https://www.hindujagruti.org/hinduism-for-kids/688.html.

Prabhavananda, Swami. *The Spiritual Heritage of India: A Clear Summary of Indian Philosophy and Religion*. Hollywood: Vedanta, 1979.

Proudfoot, Wayne. *William James and a Science of Religions: Reexperiencing "The Varieties of Religious Experience."* New York: Columbia University Press, 2004.

Qara'i, Ali Quli, trans. *The Qur'an: With a Phrase-by-Phrase English Translation*. New York: Tahrike Tarsile Qur'an, 2011.

Rabia. *Doorkeeper of the Heart of Rabia*. Translated by Charles Upton. Putney, VT: Threshold Books, 1988.

Radharkrishnan, S., trans. *The Principal Upanisads*. Daryaganj, New Delhi: Indus HarperCollins, 1994.

Ransom, Jai Ram. *It All Abides in Love: Maharajji Neem Karoli Baba*. Taos, NM: Taos Music & Art, 2014.

Rendle, Gilbert R. "Reclaiming Professional Jurisdiction: The Emergence of the Theological Task of Ministry." *ThTo* 59, no.3 (October 2002) 408–20.

Renou, Louis, ed. *Hinduism*. New York: George Braziller, 1962.

Ruether, Rosemary Radford. *Visionary Women: Three Medieval Mystics*. Minneapolis: Fortress, 2002.

Rohr, Fr. Richard, and Mike Morrell. *The Divine Dance: The Trinity and Your Transformation*. New Kensington, PA: Whitaker House, 2016.

Rosenstein, Joseph G., trans. *Siddur Eit Ratzon*. Highland Park, NJ: Shiviti, 2006.

Roth, Andrew Gabriel. *Aramaic English New Testament*. n.p. Netzari, 2008.

BIBLIOGRAPHY

Royle, Roger, and Gary Woods. *Mother Teresa: A Life in Pictures.* San Francisco: HarperCollins, 1992.

Rumi, Jalaluddin. *Rumi: In the Arms of the Beloved.* Translated by Jonathan Starr. New York: Penguin Putman, 1997.

Rutt, Stephanie. *An Ordinary Life Transformed: Lessons for Everyone from the Bhagavad Gita.* Brookline, NH: Hobblebush, 2006.

Sacks, Jonathan. "The Sound of Silence (Bamidbar 5776)." http://www.rabbisacks.org/sound-silence-bamidbar-5776.

Saint-Exupery, Antoine de. *The Little Prince.* Translated by Richard Howard. New York: Harcourt, 2000.

Saraswati, Swami Dayannanda. *Bhagavadgita Home Study Program.* Saylorsburg, PA: Arsha Vidya Gurukulam, 1989.

Satchidananda, Sri Swami. "The Function of the Mantra Prayer." *Cross Currents* 24, no. 2–3 (Sum-Fall 1974) 332–48.

———. *The Living Gita: The Complete Bhagavad Gita and Commentary.* New York: Henry Holt, 1988.

Scherman, Nosson and Meir Zlotowitz, eds. *Interlinear Chumash: The Torah, Haftaros and Five Megillos with Interlinear Translation and a Commentary Anthologized from the Rabbinic Writings.* Brooklyn, NY: Mesorah, 2013.

———. *Tehillim: The Book of Psalms with an Interlinear Translation.* Brooklyn, NY: Mesorah, 2013.

Schleiermacher, Friedrich. *On Religion: Speeches to its Cultured Despisers.* Cambridge Texts in the History of Philosophy. Translated by/Edited by Richard Crouter. Cambridge, United Kingdom: Cambridge University Press, 2015.

———. *Selected Sermons of Schleiermacher.* Translated by Mary F. Wilson. Eugene, OR: Wipf and Stock, 2004.

Shakespeare, William. *As You Like It.* Edited by Susan L. Rattiner. Mineola, NY: Dover, 1998.

Sharify-Funk, Meena and William Rory Dickson. "Traces of Panentheism in Islam: Ibn al 'Arabi and the Kaleidoscope of Being." In *Panentheism across the World's Traditions,* edited by Loriliai Biernacki and Philip Clayton, 142–60. New York: Oxford University Press, 2014.

Sherblom, Jim. "What Makes Your Heart Sing?" Lecture, Andover Newton Theological School, Newton Centre, MA, March 23, 2016.

Smith, Huston. *The World's Religions: Our Great Wisdom Traditions.* San Francisco: HarperCollins, 1991.

Spong, John Shelby. *The Sins of Scripture: Exposing the Bible's Texts of Hate to Revea the God of Love.* San Francisco: HarperCollins, 2005.

Stone, Donald. "New Religious Consciousness and Personal Religious Experience." *Sociological Analysis* 39, no.2 (Summer 1978) 123–34.

Tagore, Rabindranath. "Quotes & Quips." *Hinduism Today* October (2015) 14. http://www.hinduismtoday.com/modules/smartsection/item.php>itemid=5630.

Teilhard de Chardin, Pierre. "Christ in All Things." In *Modern Spiritual Masters,* edited by Ursula King, 82–120. Maryknoll, NY: Orbis, 1999.

BIBLIOGRAPHY

Teresa of Avila. *Interior Castle: St. Teresa of Avila.* Translated by E. Allison Peers. Mineola, NY: Dover, 2007.

Therese of Lisieux. *The Poetry of Saint Therese of Lisieux.* Translated by Donald Kinney. Washington, DC: ICS, 1996.

Twyan, James F. with Anakha Coman. *The Proof: A 40-Day Program for Embodying Oneness.* n.p. Hay House, 2009.

Vardey, Lucinda, ed. *Mother Teresa: A Simple Path.* New York: Ballantine, 1995.

Wiesel, Elie. *Night.* New York: Bantam, 1982.

Williams, Cyril G. *Basic Themes in the Comparative Study of Religion.* Lewiston, NY: Edwin Mellen, 1992.

Williams, Robert R. *Schleiermacher the Theologian: The Construction of the Doctrine of God.* Philadelphia: Fortress Press, 1978.

Young, Robin Darling. "Holy Women: Their Spiritual Influence in the Middle Ages." In *Spiritual Traditions for the Contemporary Church,* edited by Robin Maas and Gabriel O'Donnell, 396–417. Nashville, TN: Abingdon, 1990.

Zizioulas, John D. *Being as Communion: Studies in Personhood and the Church.* Crestwood, NY: St. Vladimir's Seminary, 1985.

Index

Abba, 58–59, 93, 103–4
Adhan, 108
Akandananda, Swami, 54
Al-Ahad, 88–89
Aleph-Beis, 47–48, 51, 59
al-furqaan, 63
Allah, 21, 31, 40, 60, 62–63, 79, 105–8
Allen, James, 83
al-nujmaan, 63
"Amazing Grace," 22
Amidah (Standing Prayer), 86
Ansari of Herat, 14, 45
Aramaic English New Testament (Roth), 58
Arjuna, 4–5, 7, 19, 34, 68, 85, 100–101
Artson, R. Bradley Shavit, 20, 30
As You Like It (Shakespeare), 4
As-Samad, 88–89
AUM (OM), 99–102, 110
Awoon dwashmaya, 103–5, 110

Baal Shem Tov, 48
Baptism, 22, 90
baqa, 63
Beatitudes, the, 45
Beck, Guy L., 51–52
Beloved (God)
    brick and mortar, 51
    clarity as critical to sounding our note, 87
    conclusion, 110–11
    the crucible of transcendence, 27–28
    a cry for unity, 9
    the Divine chorus, 95–96
    echoes from perennial philosophy, 14, 16
    finding God in the gallows, 43–44
    getting tuned, 44–45
    gratitude as critical to sounding our note, 90
    joy as critical to sounding our note, 86
    Love as second component in the *Sonic Trilogy of Love*, 46–47
    Lovers as first component in the *Sonic Trilogy of Love*, 37–38
    panentheism: emerging philosophical worldview, 18, 20–21, 23
    the piercing, 57–59
    the role of silence, 34–36
    the root of perfection: the number 3, 29–32
    sacred sound practices in Christianity, 103–4
    sacred sound practices in Hinduism, 100–102

Index

Beloved (continued)
 the sound of God, 54, 56
 sounding our note, 83–84
 surrender as critical to sounding our note, 92–93
 taking off our sandals, 38, 40
 as third component in the *Sonic Trilogy of Love*, 65–80
Bhagavad Gita, 4–5, 19, 32, 37, 68, 85, 100
Bible, 4–5, 46–47, 50–51, 58
Biernacki, Loriliai, 19
Big Bang, 22
bija, 54–55
Blind Men and the Elephant, 21
Borg, Marcus, 18
Boulder, Colorado, 22
Brahman, 53, 99–101
Brockopp, Jonathan E., 79
Buddhism, 13
Buna, 41

Cahalan, Kathleen A., 85
Cardenal, Ernesto, 22
Carlebach, R. Shlomo, 99
Carver, George Washington, 10–11, 14–15, 22, 79, 99
Catherine of Siena, 43
Catholicism, 22, 69
Christian Mantras: The Rediscovery and Power of an Ancient Approach to Inner Transformation (Grassi), 58
Christianity
 a cry for unity, 3, 7–8
 the Divine chorus, 96
 a Divine discourse, 64
 echoes from perennial philosophy, 15
 finding God in the gallows, 42
 Love as second component in the *Sonic Trilogy of Love*, 47

panentheism: emerging philosophical worldview, 18, 21, 23
 the piercing, 56, 58
 the root of perfection: the number 3, 28–30
 sacred sound practices in, 102–5
 seeing with new eyes, 75
 surrender as critical to sounding our note, 93
Clayton, Philip, 21, 69
The Cloud of Unknowing, 35, 56–57
Code of Jewish Law (Maimonides), 30
Cohen, Alan, 84
The Color Purple (Walker), 21
Cordovero, R. Moshe, 13, 30

Dao, the, 13, 21
Darjeeling, India, 6
De Trinitate (St. Augustine), 29
Degel Machneh Ephraim (R. Moshe Chaim Ephraim), 51
Dexter Avenue Baptist Church, 77
dharma, 85
dhikr, 107
Dhikr: The Remembrance of God (Muhaiyaddeen), 62
Dov Ber, R. (Maggid of Mezritch), 48
Drona, 100
Duryodhana, 100–101

Eastern Orthodox Church, 28
 Eastern Church, 29
Eaton, Charles Le Gai, 60
Eckhart, Meister, 4, 13, 35, 89, 91
Egypt, 5
Ein Sof, 30–31
Empedocles, 9
Errico, Rocco A., 58, 103–4
Europe, 97
Ezekiel, 87
fana, 63

Index

Fowler, Jeaneane, 19
Franciscanism, 93
"The Function of the Mantra Prayer" (Satchidananda), 44–45
A Furious Longing for God (Manning), 93

Gabriel, 60
Gandhi, Mahatma, 91
Gibran, Kahlil, 68
God
   Beloved as third component in the *Sonic Trilogy of Love*, 65–80
   brick and mortar, 47–51
   conclusion, 109–11
   the crucible of transcendence, 27–28
   a cry for unity, 3–9
   the Divine chorus, 95–96
   a Divine discourse, 60–62, 64
   echoes from perennial philosophy, 13–17
   finding in the gallows, 41–44
   getting tuned, 44–45
   gratitude as critical to sounding our note, 89–90
   harmonic preludes, 10–11
   joy as critical to sounding our note, 85–87
   Love as second component in the *Sonic Trilogy of Love*, 46–47
   love defined, 32
   Lovers as first component in the *Sonic Trilogy of Love*, 37–38
   panentheism: emerging philosophical worldview, 18–23
   the piercing, 57, 59
   the role of silence, 35
   the root of perfection: the number 3, 30–31
   sacred sound practices in Christianity, 103–5
   sacred sound practices in Hinduism, 100–101
   sacred sound practices in Islam, 105–8
   sacred sound practices in Judaism, 96–99
   the sound of, 51–56
   sounding our note, 83–84
   surrender as critical to sounding our note, 91–94
   taking off our sandals, 38–41
Golden Rule, 70
Gospels, the, 34, 102–3
Goswami, Suta, 54
Grassi, Joseph A., 58, 103
Green, R. Arthur, 73, 85, 98

Hadewijch, 7
Hadith Qudsi, 27, 40, 62
Hadith, 70
Hafiz, 68
Hartshorne, Charles, 18
Hasidic Judaism, 99
Heschel, R. Abraham Joshua, 3–4, 72
Heyward, Carter, 29, 33
Hildegard of Bingen, 35
Hinduism
   a cry for unity, 4–5, 7–8
   a Divine discourse, 63
   echoes from perennial philosophy, 13
   getting tuned, 44
   gratitude as critical to sounding our note, 90
   Love as second component in the *Sonic Trilogy of Love*, 47
   panentheism: emerging philosophical worldview, 21
   the piercing, 57
   the root of perfection: the number 3, 32

Index

Hinduism (continued)
   sacred sound practices in, 99–102
   seeing with new eyes, 73–75
   the sound of God, 51–52, 55
Hitti, Philip, 61
Holocaust, 97
Holy Spirit, 3, 29, 42, 92
Homilies on the First Epistle of John (St. Augustine), 32
Hope, Ronald, 17
hu, 63–64, 67, 106–7, 110
Hurston, Zora Neale, 67
Huxley, Aldous, 12–13, 15–17, 91

Ibn al-'Arabi, 27, 31, 107
India, 91
Interior Castle, 59
The Interlinear Chumash (Scherman and Zlotowitz), 50
Isaiah, 86
Islam, 7, 47, 59–61, 105–8
Islam and the Destiny of Man (Eaton), 60
Ismi-Azam, 64
Israelites, 5

James, William, 12, 15–16
Jesus Christ
   clarity as critical to sounding our note, 87
   the crucible of transcendence, 28
   a cry for unity, 7
   the Divine chorus, 96
   echoes from perennial philosophy, 14
   harmonic preludes, 11
   joy as critical to sounding our note, 85
   love defined, 33–34
   one and all, 68, 70
   the piercing, 58
   sacred sound practices in Christianity, 102–5
   seeing with new eyes, 75–78
   surrender as critical to sounding our note, 93
John, 102
Judah the Prince, R., 97
Judaism
   a cry for unity, 7
   a Divine discourse, 63
   joy as critical to sounding our note, 86
   Love as second component in the *Sonic Trilogy of Love*, 47
   panentheism: emerging philosophical worldview, 20
   the piercing, 57
   the root of perfection: the number 3, 30
   sacred sound practices in, 96–99
   seeing with new eyes, 72
   the sound of God, 51, 53
Julian of Norwich, 42, 78

Kabir, 11
Kadosh Kadosh Kadosh, 86–87
Kahaneman, R. Yosef, 97
kalimah, 106
Kayser, Hans, 56
Keating, Thomas, 42, 56–57
Keller, Catherine, 20
Khadija, 7
Khan, Hazrat Inayat, 46, 64, 88
King Jr., Martin Luther, 75–78
kol demamah dakah, 49, 53, 57, 63, 67, 98, 110
Krause, Karl Christian Friedrich, 18
Krishna, 5, 19, 68, 85, 100

La illaha illa Allah, 105–8, 110
Lalla Ded, 100
Law of the Last Thought, 91
The Living Gita: The Complete Bhagavad and Commentary (Satchidananda), 32, 100
Lord's Prayer, 102–3
Lossky, Vladimir, 39

124

Index

Love (sacred sound)
  Beloved as third component in the *Sonic Trilogy of Love*, 65–66
  conclusion, 110–11
  the crucible of transcendence, 27
  a cry for unity, 9
  the Divine chorus, 96
  echoes from perennial philosophy, 14, 16
  finding God in the gallows, 43
  getting tuned, 44–45
  Lovers as first component in the *Sonic Trilogy of Love*, 38
  one and all, 66, 68
  panentheism: emerging philosophical worldview, 18, 21, 23
  the role of silence, 36
  the root of perfection: the number 3, 29, 31
  sacred sound practices in Islam, 107–8
  as second component in the *Sonic Trilogy of Love*, 46–64
Lovers (practitioners)
  Beloved as third component in the *Sonic Trilogy of Love*, 65–66
  brick and mortar, 51
  clarity as critical to sounding our note, 87–88
  conclusion, 109–11
  the crucible of transcendence, 27
  a cry for unity, 9
  the Divine chorus, 95–96
  a Divine discourse, 64
  echoes from perennial philosophy, 14, 16
  as first component in the *Sonic Trilogy of Love*, 37–45
  gratitude as critical to sounding our note, 90
  Love as second component in the *Sonic Trilogy of Love*, 46–47
  love defined, 33
  one and all, 66, 68
  panentheism: emerging philosophical worldview, 18, 20–21, 23
  the piercing, 59
  the root of perfection: the number 3, 29, 31
  sacred sound practices in Christianity, 103–5
  sacred sound practices in Hinduism, 100
  sacred sound practices in Islam, 106–8
  sacred sound practices in Judaism, 98–99
  seeing with new eyes, 72, 80
  the sound of God, 52, 54–55
  sounding our note, 84
Luther, Martin, 85, 92

Maggid of Mezritch (R. Dov Ber), 48
Mahabharata, 69
Maimonides (Rambam), 30, 50–51
Manning, Brennan, 93
Mecca, Saudi Arabia, 6, 78, 80
Mechthild of Magdeburg, 18
Mevlevi Sufism, 107
Meyer, Wali Ali, 63
Michelangelo, 44
Missionaries of Charity, 6
Moses, 4–5, 7, 38–39, 50
Moshe Chaim Ephraim, R., 51
Mother Mary, 34
Mother Teresa, 4–7, 69, 75–76
Mother Teresa (DVD), 75
Mount Hira, 6, 59
Mount Sinai, 39

Index

Muhaiyaddeen, M. R. Bawa, 61–62, 106
Muhammad, 4, 6–7, 59–60, 62, 78–80, 108
Munk, R. Michael L., 47–48, 50–51, 97
The Mystical Theology of the Eastern Church (Lossky), 39

nada, 53–54, 56–57, 63, 67, 101–2, 110
Nazism, 41
Neem Karoli Baba, 74
New Testament, 4, 18, 103
Night (Wiesel), 41
Night of Power, 60
Nobel Peace Prize, 77
Noohra Foundation, 58
nothingness and nowhere, 57, 64, 67, 105, 110

Of Human Freedom (Schelling), 18
Ohar, Abu, 40
Olson, Roger E., 22
OM (AUM), 99–102, 110
Open Mind, Open Heart (Keating), 42
An Ordinary Life Transformed: Lessons for Everyone from the Bhagavad Gita (Rutt), 44

Palestine, 58
Panentheism, 17–23
Panentheism across World Traditions (Biernacki), 19
Parliament of World Religions, 7
Patterson, Kerry, 88
Pedro Arrupe, Father, 69
Pharaoh, 5
Plato, 45
Porete, Marguerite, 65
"A Postconservative Evangelical Response to Panentheism" (Olson), 22

Promised Land, 77
Pseudo-Dionysius, 39

Qara'i, Ali Quli, 61
Qur'an
 a cry for unity, 4, 6–8
 a Divine discourse, 60–62
 joy as critical to sounding our note, 85
 panentheism: emerging philosophical worldview, 21
 the root of perfection: the number 3, 31
 sacred sound practices in Islam, 107
 seeing with new eyes, 79
The Qur'an: With a Phrase-by-Phrase English Translation, 61

Rabia, 95
Raja, C. Kunhan, 52
Rama, 90–91
Rambam (Maimonides), 30, 50–51
The Redemption of God: A Theology of Mutual Relation (Heyward), 33
Rendle, Gilbert R., 84
Rohr, Father Richard, 66
Rolle, Richard, 96
Roth, Andrew Gabriel, 58
Royal Secret, 19
Ruether, Rosemary Radford, 78
Rumi, Jalaluddin, 13, 34, 40, 64, 95, 106–8

Saadiah Gaon, R., 72–73
Sacks, R. Jonathan, 49–50
Saint Teresa. *See* Mother Teresa
Saint-Exupéry, Antione de, 74
Saraswati, Swami Dayananda, 102
Satchidananda, Sri Swami, 32, 44–45, 51, 85, 100, 102
Sat-Chit-Ananda, 102
sattva, 44

Index

Schelling, Friedrich, 18
Scherman, R. Nosson, 50
Schleiermacher, Friedrich, 12,
    14–16, 84
Scott, Bernard Brandon, 103
Self, the
    finding God in the gallows, 43
    getting tuned, 45
    gratitude as critical to sounding
        our note, 90
    Lovers as first component in the
        Sonic Trilogy of Love, 38
    one and all, 68
    the role of silence, 35
    sacred sound practices in
        Hinduism, 101
    sacred sound practices in Islam,
        106, 108
*Setting a Trap for God: The Aramaic
    Prayer of Jesus* (Errico), 58
shabda, 53–54, 56
Shabistari, Mahmud, 107
Shakespeare, William, 4
Shema, 50, 96–99, 110
Shneur Zalman of Liadi, R., 48
Showings (Julian of Norwich), 42
Shulhan Arukh, 97
Siddur, 97
sifat, 63
The Sins of Scripture (Spong), 104
Sisters of Loreto, 6
Sixteenth Street Baptist Church, 76
Smith, Huston, 60–61
Society of Jesus, 69
*Sonic Theology: Hinduism and
    Sacred Sound* (Beck), 51
Sonic Trilogy of Love
    Beloved as third component in
        the *Sonic Trilogy of Love*,
        65–66
    conclusion, 109–10
    the crucible of transcendence,
        27–28
    a cry for unity, 9
    the Divine chorus, 95

echoes from perennial
    philosophy, 12–17
harmonic preludes, 11–12
Love as second component in
    the *Sonic Trilogy of Love*, 47
love defined, 32–33
Lovers as first component in the
    Sonic Trilogy of Love, 37–38
one and all, 66–67, 70
panentheism: emerging
    philosophical worldview, 18,
    20, 23
the root of perfection: the
    number 3, 29–31
seeing with new eyes, 71
"The Sound of Silence" (Sacks), 49
Spiritual Canticle (St. John of the
    Cross), 40
Spong, John Shelby, 104
St. Anselm, 12
St. Augustine, 29–30, 32, 39, 67,
    69, 71
St. Catherine of Genoa, 11
St. Dionysius, 27
St. Francis of Assisi, 35, 40
St. Gregory Nazianzen, 28, 45
St. John of the Cross, 34, 40
St. Maynard School of Theology, 103
St. Teresa of Ávila, 37–38, 59, 84
St. Therese of Lisieux, 11
Standing Prayer (Amidah), 86
Stone, Donald, 66
Strong, Augustus Hopkins, 22
Sufism, 13, 31, 40, 46, 88–89, 106–7
Superman, 76
The Survey of Sanskrit Literature
    (Raja), 52
svadharma, 85

Tagore, Rabindranath, 8
Talmud, 50, 69, 97
Taraka, 91
tat tvam asi, 13, 32, 52, 54, 100
tawhid, 31, 106
Teilhard de Chardin, Pierre, 75

INDEX

Their Eyes Were Watching God (Hurston), 67
Thirteen Principles of Faith, 50
tikkun 'olam, 85
Torah, 8, 48, 50
Tree of Life Interfaith Seminary, 41
Trinity, 28–30, 66, 78
Truth, 21–22, 32, 43, 52, 60

Unity, 58
University of Colorado, 22
Unknown, the, 38–39
Upanisads, the, 52, 74, 99–100

Vak, 52
The Varieties of Religious Experience (James), 16
Vedas, the, 51–54, 91

Walker, Alice, 21
wazifah, 8, 88–89
Whirling Dervishes, 107
Wiesel, Elie, 41
Williams, Cyril G., 53
Williams, Robert R., 14

Yesodei ha-Torah, 30

Zizioulas, John D., 87
Zlotowitz, R. Meir, 50

www.ingramcontent.com/pod-product-compliance
Lightning Source LLC
Chambersburg PA
CBHW072146160426
43197CB00012B/2264